90 Days Bible Reading Guide

GW00384110

SPIRITUALITY

MANY THANKS TO THE ORIGINAL
AM/PM TEAM, TO JOHN BUCKERIDGE
FOR ACTING AS CONSULTANT
EDITOR, TO PHIL WASON AND PAUL
FENTON FOR THEIR ADVICE AND
SUPPORT AND TO PHIL JONES AT
WALDON WHITE JONES FOR HIS
DESIGN.

ACKNOWLEDGEMENTS

90 DAYS BIBLE READING GUIDE

Scripture Union
207–209 Queensway, Bletchley
Milton Keynes MK2 2EB.
Email: info@scriptureunion.org.uk
Website: www.scriptureunion.org.uk

Scripture Union Australia
Locked Bag 2, Central Coast Business Centre, NSW 2252
Website: www.su.org.au

Scripture Union USA
P.O.Box 987, Valley Forge, PA 19482
Website: www.scriptureunion.org

Design by Waldon White Jones
Printed in Great Britain by
Goodman Baylis & Son Limited
The Trinity Press, Worcester, and London.

ISBN 1 84427 046 7

Scripture Union is an international Christian charity working with
churches in more than 130 countries, providing resources to bring the
good news about Jesus Christ to children, young people and families -
and to encourage them to develop spiritually through the Bible and
prayer.

As well as our network of volunteers, staff and associates who run
holidays, church-based events and school Christian groups, we
produce a wide range of publications and support those who use
resources through training programmes.

CONFUSED?

start here!

DAYZD is a Bible Reading Guide that you can start whenever you like and read wherever you like!

DAYZD gets to the heart of what the Bible says about *worship*. It won't give you all the theological answers, but it will encourage you to think about what the Bible says for yourself.

What to do?

• **Pray before you start.** If you ask God to speak to you as you use DAYZD he will!

• **Read the Bible passage.** Ask yourself: What is the main point of the passage? What does the Bible passage say about God? Have I learnt something new about myself? Is there a promise or a warning to take notice of?

• **Read DAYZD.**

• **Make notes.** There is some space on each page to jot down any thoughts or comments you have on the passage.

• **Pray.** After you have finished each study, talk to God about how you feel and what you have learnt.

• **Action.** Check out the 'Action' section which includes prayer ideas, song lyrics to meditate on, worship ideas, books to read and quotes to think about.

• **Tick box.** On each page there is a small 'tick box'. When you feel you have completed a page, tick the box. This will help you remember where you are in your DAYZD Bible Reading Guide.

• DAYZD is based on the *Good News Bible*, but can be used with other Bible translations.

MATTHEW 6:9a

'OUR FATHER'. THE INTIMATE WAY IN WHICH JESUS SPOKE ABOUT GOD AS HIS FATHER WAS ONE OF THE MOST REVOLUTIONARY THINGS ABOUT HIS TEACHING. HOW FULLY DO *YOU* EXPERIENCE GOD AS YOUR HEAVENLY FATHER? THIS MEDITATION ON THE OPENING OF THE LORD'S PRAYER IS DESIGNED TO HELP YOU EXPLORE GOD'S FATHERHOOD.

Take a few moments to think about the following questions and write down on a piece of paper any thoughts you have:

• What qualities do you think make a good parent; loving? caring? protecting? dependable? Add any others you can think of.

• Would a good parent discipline his children? If so, when?

After thinking about these questions spend some time considering your relationship with your own parents or someone who looks after you. Thank God for the good qualities they have as guardians over you.

It may be that your relationship with your parents isn't that great. It is often hard for us to relate to God as our heavenly Father when we feel that our own parents have let us down in some way. How do we know that our heavenly Father won't treat us in the same way? Although God allows us to address him as *'abba'* – an intimate address from a child to his father, God does not have any of the short comings that we humans have, he is truly perfect and will never leave us or let us down. Don't ignore any bad vibes or unhappy feelings that you have about your own background – spend time now bringing them to God for his healing.

Look at your list of what qualities make a good parent. In which ways does God fulfil those qualities for you? Thank God for this.

HOW FULLY DO YOU EXPERIENCE GOD AS YOUR HEAVENLY FATHER?

ACTION

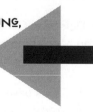

• READ *THE FATHER HEART OF GOD* BY FLOYD McCLUNG, PUBLISHED BY YWAM.

• READ ROMANS 8:16,17. WHAT DOES IT SAY ABOUT OUR RELATIONSHIP WITH GOD AND JESUS?

MATTHEW 6:9b

'MAY YOUR HOLY NAME BE HONOURED'

IT IS QUITE HARD FOR US TODAY TO UNDERSTAND WHAT THIS ACTUALLY MEANS. WE LIVE IN A SOCIETY WHERE VERY LITTLE IS TREATED AS HOLY.
An RE teacher once asked his pupils to think of anything in their daily lives which was treated as 'holy'. 'My dad's CD' was one example. 'I'm not allowed to breathe on it let alone touch it!'. The Old Testament Jews felt even more strongly about God. His name was so holy that they were not allowed to speak it.

Think about the word 'holy'. What does it mean to you? What would you consider in your life as being holy. Today, we follow the word 'holy' around the Bible to find out what being holy really means for us today.

• **THE BARRIER.** Read Leviticus 16:1-4 and 17-19. God is holy – free from all sin. Man is unholy, because he has sinned. For the Israelites to come to worship God, they had to go through all sorts of purifying ceremonies to make themselves clean. All year they would try to obey the detailed laws God had given them, and the priests would offer animal sacrifices for the people's sins. The barrier between God, and man was firmly fixed.

• **THE BARRIER BROKEN.** Read Mark 15:37,38. Why did the curtain tear when Jesus died? Hebrews 10:12 explains it and Hebrews 10:19 puts it in a nutshell. Through the perfect sacrifice Jesus made, the barrier is broken. We are free to worship God not just from afar, but actually *in* his most holy place!

• **A NEW LIFE.** So what does all of this mean for us? Doesn't God care how we live any more? No! He does care. As it says in Hebrews 10:20, Jesus has opened for us a new way, and we are called up into a new life. And so we get back to the beginning of the Lord's prayer, and honouring God's name. Doing this doesn't just mean not saying it as a swear-word. It means that if we identify with God by calling ourselves Christians, we'd better make sure we live as God wants us to live. What does he want from us? He wants us to be holy! See Colossians 1:21,22.

ACTION

• AFTER LOOKING AT THESE BIBLE REFERENCES, THINK ABOUT WHETHER YOU WOULD CONSIDER YOUR OWN LIFE AS HOLY AND PLEASING TO GOD. ARE THERE THINGS IN YOUR LIFE THAT YOU KNOW GOD WOULDN'T FIND PLEASING AND WHICH ARE AFFECTING YOUR WORSHIP OF HIM? JOT THESE DOWN ON A SCRAP OF PAPER. LOOK AT EACH ONE AND THEN ASK GOD TO HELP YOU TO DEAL WITH THEM. WHEN YOU HAVE FINISHED, SCREW THE PAPER UP AND THROW IT AWAY. THIS IS WHAT GOD WILL DO WITH THESE PROBLEMS AS WELL.

DAYZD 2

CHECK OUT
MATTHEW 6:10

'MAY YOUR KINGDOM COME'. WHAT KINGDOM? WHEN? WHERE? HOW? FIND OUT BY READING MATTHEW 6:10 AND FOLLOWING THIS WORD STUDY:

1. Isaiah 9:6,7. God promises a kingdom that will never end. Who is going to bring it about?

Pick out the words which show how it is going to be different from other kingdoms.

2. Matthew 4:17 and 23. Jesus announces the kingdom. How did he show that God's power was at work through him?

3. Matthew 5:3. Perhaps this verse is a bit surprising. But then, Jesus' kingdom is radically different from earthly kingdoms. What do you think 'spiritually poor' means?

WHEN?
WHERE?
HOW?

4. Matthew 7:21. What's the connection between 'May your Kingdom come' and 'May your will be done'?

5. John 3:3. How much does our outlook have to change before we can see God's Kingdom? What might 'seeing' God's kingdom mean?

6. Matthew 13:24-30,36-43. Is the Kingdom of God:
• completely separate from the world?
• happening within the world?
• completely in the future?
• already begun, but not yet complete?

As far as you can remember, write down everything you spent time on during the last week (leave out sleeping, washing and eating). Where can you see God's kingdom at work in your life? In other words, how much is your life being affected by God's values of peace, justice, righteousness? Are there specific areas you want to ask God's kingdom to come into? Bring them to him now.

ACTION

'THE KINGDOM OF GOD' WAS A PHRASE JESUS USED OFTEN. IF YOU HAVE TIME, SPEED-READ MATTHEW'S GOSPEL AND NOTE DOWN HOW MANY TIMES AND IN WHAT CONTEXT 'THE KINGDOM OF GOD' IS MENTIONED.

MATTHEW 6:11

'I AM THE BREAD OF LIFE,' SAID JESUS (JOHN 6:35), JUST AFTER HE HAD FED FIVE THOUSAND PEOPLE BY A MIRACLE. DID HE MEAN THAT HIS FOLLOWERS WOULD NEVER RUN SHORT OF FOOD? AND IF WE HAVE AMPLE FOOD DOES THAT MEAN THAT WE CAN IGNORE THIS VERSE?

Human beings need more than food and drink to keep them alive (Matthew 4:4). We need to love and be loved, to feel that we are worth something, to be creative in work and leisure. Most of all we need to relate to God, because that is what we were made for.

To lead you into meditating on Matthew 6:11, write down some of the basic things you need (not what you would quite like, but what you really need – bread represents the necessities of life not the luxuries!).

• In order to stay alive and healthy, I need ...
• In order to feel life is worthwhile, I need ...
• In order to become more like Jesus and worship him, I need ...

Now think of everything you know you've got to do today or tomorrow. In your head, slowly 'walk through' your day with Jesus beside you (if you find it helpful, close your eyes). As you get to each part of the day that you've got to face, tell Jesus what you need to face that situation, eg wisdom, courage, patience. Remember it doesn't matter how small or insignificant we think the task is, Jesus is willing to help us through it.

When you have brought your needs for the day to God, thank him for knowing what you need even better than you do. Ask him to guide you by his Spirit so that you know what you need and what you don't!

ACTION

READ GEORGE MÜLLER'S STORY IN *GEORGE MÜLLER*, BY BASIL MILLER, PUBLISHED BY BETHANY HOUSE.

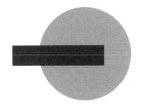

MATTHEW 6:12a

'I'D LIKE TO FORGIVE BUT I CAN'T!'

HAVE YOU EVER HEARD THE PHRASE 'I CAN FORGIVE BUT I CAN'T FORGET'? WHAT THIS USUALLY MEANS IS THAT 'I'D LIKE TO FORGIVE BUT I CAN'T OR WON'T!' FORGIVING IS HARD WORK. MAYBE THAT IS WHY JESUS WENT BACK OVER THE IMPORTANCE OF FORGIVENESS IN VERSES 14,15 AS WELL.

Over the next two studies we look at the trouble that Peter, one of Jesus' disciples, had in understanding forgiveness. He knew Jesus wanted people to forgive each other, but surely that couldn't mean going on forgiving for ever?

Spend five minutes thinking about whether there is something or someone in your life which you are having trouble forgiving. Next, think about the things we need forgiveness for, eg bad attitude. Read Matthew 5:7 and 6:12 again. It is hard to forgive, but if we want to be forgiven we have to be prepared to forgive others. Ask God now to help you to give up the resentment you feel towards this situation

Finally, spend some time asking God to help you with your attitude. Remember that to worship God truly we have to offer our whole life to him as a living sacrifice.

ACTION

• PRAISE GOD THAT THROUGH THE DEATH OF JESUS WE HAVE ULTIMATE FORGIVENESS.

MATTHEW 6:12b

WHEN WE HAVE COMPLETELY TURNED OUR BACK ON GOD, CAN THERE EVER BE A SECOND CHANCE? PETER HAD BETRAYED JESUS WHEN JESUS MOST NEEDED FRIENDS. READ MATTHEW 18:21,22. PETER KNEW JESUS WANTED PEOPLE TO FORGIVE EACH OTHER, BUT SURELY NOT EVERY TIME?

Look at Matthew 26:31-35. Peter was so sure that he was going to be the only disciple not to turn his back on Jesus. Now turn to verses 69-75. Less than twelve hours later, Peter's promises have been forgotten. Imagine how Peter felt when he realised what he had done (v 75). Have you ever felt really ashamed of something you've done, and thought 'I can't forgive myself, so how can I ask God to forgive me?' That's how it must have been for Peter. Although Peter had denied Jesus three times, Jesus does not walk away from him. Read Acts 2:1-4,14,38,39. It is interesting to note that one of the main things Peter has to say is that Jesus forgives sins. I wonder where he learnt that?!

Spend some time thinking about whether there have been points in your life when it has been easier to deny that you know Jesus than acknowledge him. It may have been when someone challenged your faith. Denying Jesus does not have to be done verbally, we can equally deny him with our actions and the way we live our life. Ask him to forgive you for these times and ask him to give you the ability to be stronger the next time you are challenged.

• JUST AS JESUS FORGAVE PETER, SO HE WILL FORGIVE US. EVEN THE THINGS WHICH WE FEEL THAT WE CANNOT FORGIVE OURSELVES FOR, HE WILL FORGIVE. ARE THERE ANY AREAS IN YOUR LIFE WHICH YOU CANNOT FORGIVE YOURSELF FOR? TELL GOD ABOUT THESE AND ASK HIM TO HELP YOU GIVE THESE OVER TO HIM.

MATTHEW 6:13

'TEMPTATION' SIMPLY MEANS 'TESTING'.

'LEAD US NOT INTO TEMPTATION' IS THE BEST KNOWN VERSION OF VERSE 13. 'TEMPTATION' SIMPLY MEANS 'TESTING'.

A couple of years ago there was an advert in Britain for a sparkling apple drink. It was set in an imaginary Garden of Eden and focused on an 'Eve' character falling for the seductive flavour of *Appletise*, and then the equally seductive 'Adam'. It's marketing line was 'lead us not into temptation' – although I'm sure they wanted people to be tempted to buy their product. Temptation is a hard thing to resist; we are often tempted in the areas where we are weakest.

Whether we face temptation or suffering, God allows us to be tested in our faith as a way of showing our obedience to him. All of us, at some time or other, have to cope with problems, hassle, confusion and the pressures of evil around us. Praying with each other and for each other is the surest way of finding strength to cope.

As we have been focusing on prayer, why not spend some time praying for ...

• anyone you know who is having a tough time at the moment.
• anyone you know who is in danger of being led away from God by something that seems more important.
• any situation of need that's been in the world news recently.
• any group or country whose need has gone on for so long that it doesn't make the world news any more.
• any way in which you feel God might be calling you to help others.
• strength in dealing with the things that tempt you.

ACTION

• JESUS DIDN'T JUST TELL US HOW IMPORTANT IT IS TO PRAY, HE ACTUALLY DID IT HIMSELF. LOOK THROUGH MARK'S GOSPEL AND SEE HOW MANY REFERENCES YOU CAN FIND TO JESUS PRAYING.

CHECK OUT

PSALM 104:1-24,33,34

THIS PSALM STRAIGHT FROM THE PAGES OF THE JEWISH HYMN-BOOK, IS A BRILLIANT SONG OF PRAISE! IT FOCUSES ON THE CREATOR, PAINTING WORD PICTURES WITH BOLD POETIC STROKES - SEARING LIGHTNING; TOWERING, ROLLING CLOUDS. THEY ARE PICTURES OF GOD'S TREMENDOUS POWER - YET THESE WORD PICTURES HAVE THEIR PERSONAL TOUCHES TOO. AS IN THE STORY OF CREATION, WE ARE SWEPT FROM AWESOME POWER TO INTIMATE CARE, FROM HEAVEN AND EARTH (VS 1-9) TO DONKEYS, LIONS AND BIRDS (V 10 ONWARDS). GOD'S CREATION IS ORDERED, A CIRCLE OF LIFE, WITH EVERY DETAIL THOUGHT OUT, WITH PEOPLE THE MOST SPECIAL PART. AND GOD'S POWER IS STILL HOLDING IT ALL TOGETHER.

GOD'S POWER IS STILL HOLDING IT ALL TOGETHER.

• Check out Colossians 1:15-17. What is Christ's position in creation?
• Read Matthew 10:29-31. What is your position in God's creation?

Now spend some time worshipping God, thanking him for the splendour and beauty of his creation. If you are able to see something of his creation now, (eg, your garden, trees, plants, animals, sky, stars), choose one thing and focus on that with your eyes closed. If this isn't possible, choose one of the verses from the psalm and meditate on that. If you feel it is appropriate, play some music which helps you to focus on God's creation, eg 'I can sing of your love forever', *It's A Small World*, *Spring Harvest Praise Mix 1995*.

ACTION

• TRY TO WRITE YOUR OWN SONG OF PRAISE USING IMAGES FROM GOD'S CREATION. IF YOU ARE ABLE TO, WHY NOT TRY AND SET IT TO MUSIC.

DAY-Z-D 8

PSALM 29

GOD SPEAKS, THE WORLD REACTS.

BEETHOVEN ONCE WROTE A SYMPHONY THAT STARTED IN PRAISE OF NATURE, MOVED THROUGH A STORM, AND ENDED IN PEACE. PSALM 29 IS A SYMPHONY WHICH STARTS WITH AN INVITATION FOR ANGELS TO PRAISE THEIR CREATOR (V 1). THE STORM THAT FOLLOWS, STARTING OUT AT SEA AND MOVING OVER THE MOUNTAINS TO THE DESERT, IS A VIVID PICTURE OF THE POWER OF GOD (THOUGH IT'S ONLY A PALE REFLECTION OF HIS REAL POWER). EVEN HIS VOICE ALONE PROMPTS ACTION - GOD SPEAKS, THE WORLD REACTS (VS 3,4).

When we catch a glimpse of God's power, we can almost be startled by God's greatness; but we remember that he is personal too. We are to acknowledge his power and to be proud of having such a Father. When he speaks, we should react! Are you willing to?

Take some time out from the busyness of your life to sit in quietness now and listen to what God might be saying to you.

ACTION

• PLAY A PRAISE TAPE/CD (EG, THE INSTRUMENTAL TRACK OF 'LORD I LIFT YOUR NAME ON HIGH' FROM *NITRO PRAISE* [N-SOUL RECORDS]. AS THE MUSIC PLAYS IN THE BACKGROUND THINK OF ANY EXPERIENCE YOU HAVE HAD WHICH HAS SHOWN YOU THE POWER OF GOD. USE THE MUSIC TO PRAY, OUT LOUD OR IN YOUR HEAD, THANKING AND PRAISING GOD FOR HIS GREATNESS.

• READ VERSE 11 OUT LOUD, SEVERAL TIMES OVER, WITH AN INSTRUMENTAL MUSIC PLAYING IN THE BACKGROUND. MEDITATE ON ITS MEANING.

CHECK OUT
PSALM 8

TO MAKE THIS PSALM REALLY COME ALIVE, READ IT THROUGH AT NIGHT UNDER THE STARS! THIS MAY SOUND CRAZY, BUT TRY IT - IF YOU LIVE IN A PLACE WHERE THE STARS CAN STILL BE SEEN PRETTY CLEARLY, TAKE YOUR BIBLE, A TORCH AND A BLANKET AND LIE DOWN OUTSIDE ON THE GROUND LOOKING UP INTO THE NIGHT SKY. THEN READ THE PSALM THROUGH, A VERSE AT A TIME. BETWEEN VERSES LOOK AT THE STARS. LOOKING UP AT THE STARS MAKES US FEEL SMALL AND INSIGNIFICANT, BUT IN GOD'S PLAN WE WILL SHARE HIS GLORY AND HONOUR, AS RULERS WITH JESUS (VS 5,6).

Even the stars join in to worship God! A recent exploration by the Hubble telescope discovered that stars sing – not too surprising considering the book of Job mentions this amazing fact (Job 38:7). Try to imagine what kind of sound a star makes.

Praise God for his creation!

ACTION

• THE BIBLE TELLS US AS CHRISTIANS TO 'SHINE LIKE STARS LIGHTING UP THE SKY' (PHILIPPIANS 2:15). WHAT DO YOU THINK THIS MEANS?

• ARE THERE WAYS IN YOUR LIFE THAT YOU CAN SHINE MORE LIKE A STAR? SPEND TIME IN PRAYER, ASKING GOD TO SHOW YOU WAYS OF DOING THIS.

GENESIS 1:26-2:4

ONLY AFTER FIVE DAYS' HARD WORK WAS GOD READY TO SAY 'AND NOW WE WILL MAKE HUMAN BEINGS'. THIS WAS THE SPECIAL PART OF CREATION - GOD'S BEST THING. JUST AS GOD IS KING OF CREATION, SO PEOPLE WERE TO HAVE POWER OVER ANIMALS AND PLANTS. JUST AS HE HAS A MIND, THOUGHTS, FEELINGS, A WILL AND PERSONALITY, SO HAD MAN AND WOMAN. PEOPLE = GOD'S MASTERPIECE!

Christians have different ideas about whether 'a day' means 24 hours here. The important point is that God created a regular rhythm of work and rest. Our seven-day week reflects the pattern of creation. All of God's creation reflects his glory, but people in particular were made to mirror God here on earth.

Think about the following questions:

• What did God feel about what he had made? Why? Spend a few minutes taking in how God feels about *you*.

• What do you think God feels about what we've done with his world?

• What practical things can you do to look after God's world in the way that he intended us to?

ACTION

• THINK ABOUT THE CHRISTIANS YOU KNOW. IN WHAT WAYS DO THEY MIRROR CHRIST? MAKE A LIST OF ALL THE QUALITIES YOU CAN THINK OF. NOW THINK ABOUT YOUR OWN LIFE. CAN YOU SEE ANY OF THESE CHRIST-LIKE QUALITIES IN YOURSELF? TAKE SOME TIME TO THANK GOD FOR THESE PEOPLE AND PRAY THAT OTHERS MAY BE ABLE TO SEE GOD THROUGH YOUR LIFE AS WELL.

• 'MAN IS THE CREATURE MADE AT THE END OF A WEEK'S WORK WHEN GOD WAS TIRED.' *MARK TWAIN*.

THINK ABOUT THIS QUOTE. FROM WHAT YOU HAVE READ TODAY, DO YOU THINK THIS IS TRUE?

JOB 38

SOME PRETTY UNANSWERABLE QUESTIONS.

GOD, BEING GOD, POSES SOME PRETTY UNANSWERABLE QUESTIONS. IT COULDN'T BE ANY OTHER WAY. WE CAN AND SHOULD UNDERSTAND A LOT ABOUT GOD, BUT ONLY AS MUCH AS HE SHOWS US. READ ROMANS 11:33.

The questions in Job 38 are about the mysteries of creation. Science, in a different language, still asks many of them. Look at two of the questions God asks Job and circle the right answer:

• Verse 18 – can science answer this question? Yes/No.
• Verse 5 – can science answer this? Yes/No.

Science can tell us how the world is put together, but never why or by whom. If we only know about God in our heads, then we're missing out on the best bits! The good news is that he wants our hearts. He wants us to know his great love and to love him back.

NOW KEEP YOUR EYES OPEN.

Your God Is Too Small was the title of a book some years ago. Is your idea of God big enough to imagine the person who created this amazing world? Pray and ask God to show you more of his greatness today. Now keep your eyes open during the next twenty-four hours, because God is very likely to answer your prayer.

ACTION

• OVER THE NEXT MONTH READ *IT MAKES SENSE*, BY STEPHEN GAUKROGER, PUBLISHED BY SCRIPTURE UNION.

• 'YOUR GOD IS TOO SMALL'. THINK ABOUT THE WAYS IN WHICH YOU LIMIT GOD'S ABILITIY AND POWER.

DAYZD 12

CHECK OUT

REVELATION 7:9-17

THIS IS ONE OF THE MOST AMAZING AND EXCITING PASSAGES IN THE BIBLE! IMAGINE THE LARGEST GATHERING OF CHRISTIANS THAT YOU HAVE EXPERIENCED AND THEN IMAGINE A GROUP THOUSANDS AND THOUSANDS OF TIMES BIGGER - THAT'S THE KIND OF GROUP SIZE THAT THIS PASSAGE IS REFERRING TO.

Just think, not only being in the presence of God but a Countless crowd of people all worshipping God too – and giving 100 per cent! It makes the best turn-out at church look pretty pathetic! There were no 'Half-hearted Herberts' here – 'They called out in a loud voice' (v 10) and 'Then they threw themselves face downwards in front of the throne and worshipped God' (v 11).

Heaven is going to be the ultimate worship experience. What we experience on earth can only be a glimpse of what that is going to be like. Sometimes we struggle to worship God – because we are distracted by our problems and surroundings or because we have a limited view of God. In heaven we will see God in all his glory and greatness and praise will be as easy and natural as breathing. There will be nothing to distract us from doing this – no more discrimination, no more suffering in the world, no more persecution, no more famine or drought and no more pain or sadness (vs 9,14-17).

What do you think it is going to be like in heaven? Read through Revelation 7:9-17 again. However good you think it is going to be, one thing you can be sure of – it's going to be even better!

ACTION

• USE VERSES 14-17 TO MEDITATE ON. THINK ABOUT THE CHRISTIANS YOU KNOW WHO ARE PERSECUTED IN THIS WORLD. MAYBE YOU FEEL PERSECUTED YOURSELF FOR WHAT YOU BELIEVE. THIS PASSAGE IS A REAL ENCOURAGEMENT TO ALL OF US. PRAY THAT GOD WILL GIVE ALL THOSE WHO ARE BEING PERSECUTED FOR WORSHIPPING HIM, STRENGTH TO HOLD ON TO THEIR FAITH AND TRUST THAT HE WILL PROTECT THEM.

PSALM 139

PSALM 139 DEMONSTRATES THAT GOD IS THERE FOR US IN THE BAD TIMES AS WELL AS THE GOOD. THIS PSALM DEMANDS HONESTY AND REALITY IN OUR FRIENDSHIP WITH GOD. HE DOESN'T ALLOW ANY 'SKELETON IN THE CUPBOARD' TACTICS; IT WON'T WASH, BECAUSE NOTHING IS HIDDEN FROM HIM!

GOD IS THERE FOR US IN THE BAD TIMES AS WELL AS THE GOOD.

But how can a perfect God, who knows us through and through still care for us? God's care for us doesn't come from seeing only our best. He knows everything about us, good and bad. Total knowledge, and yet total love; accepting us as we are, and yet loving us enough to change the things in us that are damaging our relationship with him. Even on our off days when we wish he wasn't around, he is faithful (2 Timothy 2:13).

Read aloud verses 1-18,23,24 and spend some time meditating on these. Finally offer to God the things which are causing you pain at the moment, and pray for his help in dealing with them.

ACTION

• ON A PIECE OF PAPER LIST THREE THINGS YOU WOULD RATHER GOD DIDN'T KNOW ABOUT YOU. RE-READ VERSES 23 AND 24.

PSALM 16

THINK ABOUT THE PEOPLE YOU KNOW - YOUR FRIENDS, FAMILY, ETC. OUT OF ALL OF THEM, WHO WOULD YOU SAY IS THE MOST COMMITTED TO GOD? NOW THINK ABOUT ALL THE PEOPLE WHO LIVE OR HAVE LIVED IN THIS WORLD. OUT OF EVERYBODY WHO IS *THE* ONE MOST COMMITTED TO GOD? WHAT ABOUT IN THE BIBLE - WHO SHOWS THE MOST COMMITMENT THERE?

As any good youth leader will tell you the answer has to be Jesus – but why? Take some time to ponder why Christ's commitment is greater than any person who has lived or will live. Check out Acts 2:29-36 where it refers to King David, the person who wrote this psalm, and explains Christ's commitment to God and to us.

To be able to worship God fully, we have to be totally committed to him. Can you apply this psalm personally? Verse 5 sums it all up. Is God all you have, or do you hold on to 'other gods' (v 4)? Look at the progression of ideas. Knowing God better (vs 1-3) leads to deeper commitment. Commitment leads to security in God (vs 5,8), guidance (v 7), gifts (v 6), joy, pleasure (v 11), and protection (v 9). Can't be bad!

WORSHIP GOD FULLY.

ACTION

• 'GOD OF GOODNESS, GIVE ME YOURSELF; FOR YOU ARE SUFFICIENT FOR ME. I CANNOT PROPERLY ASK ANYTHING LESS, TO BE WORTHY OF YOU. IF I WERE TO ASK LESS, I SHOULD BE ALWAYS IN WANT. IN YOU ALONE DO I HAVE ALL,' *DAME JULIAN OF NORWICH (A 14TH CENTURY NUN).*

• THIS PSALM ALSO TELLS US THAT GOD GUIDES US (VS 7,8). IS THERE A DECISION WHICH YOU ARE HAVING TO MAKE AT THE MOMENT? PRAY THAT GOD MAY GUIDE YOU IN THE DIRECTION THAT HE WANTS YOU TO GO, AND THAT YOU MAY ALWAYS BE AWARE OF HIS PRESENCE.

PSALM 91

THERE'S S𝒪METHIN𝒢 UNUSUAL AB𝒪UT PSALM 91. LIKE A FEW 𝒪THER PSALMS, IT HAS M𝒪RE THAN 𝒪NE PERS𝒪N TAKIN𝒢 PART. IN FA𝒞T, THERE ARE THREE INV𝒪LVED: FIRST, THE 'LISTENER', SEC𝒪ND THE 'SPEAKER' (VS 1-13) AND THIRD, G𝒪D HIMSELF (VS 14-16).

'IT'S ALL VERY WELL F𝒪R Y𝒪U T𝒪 HAVE FAITH,

BUT IT D𝒪ESN'T W𝒪RK F𝒪R ME!'

'IT'S ALL VERY WELL F𝒪R Y𝒪U T𝒪 HAVE FAITH,

It's as though the 'listener' has made the old comment: 'It's all very well for you to have faith, but it doesn't work for me!' The psalm is an answer to that, and it is very persuasive. Look at the word 'whoever' which comes twice in verse 1. The 'speaker' makes God's care very possible and very personal. No matter what happens or who else ignores God, you can know his care. Then God himself makes the same promise: 'I will ... I will ... I will'.

• Does the psalm say that those who follow God will never have any troubles? If not, what does it say? Check out verse 15.

• What help can this psalm be to someone who is in the middle of major difficulties?

ACTION

• THINK 𝒪F ANY W𝒪RRIES 𝒪R FEARS Y𝒪U MI𝒢HT HAVE. READ THR𝒪U𝒢H THE PSALM A𝒢AIN AND SEE H𝒪W G𝒪D WANTS T𝒪 BE WITH Y𝒪U IN THESE AND SPEND S𝒪ME TIME LETTIN𝒢 THIS SINK IN.

DAYZD 16

PSALMS 42 & 43

HAVE YOU EVER FELT A MILLION MILES AWAY FROM GOD? EVENTS GETTING YOU DOWN? PEOPLE HASSLING YOU? YOUR BIBLE GATHERING DUST. PRAYERS BOUNCING OFF THE CEILING? FEELING THAT YOU MAY NEVER HAVE THE WILL TO WORSHIP GOD AGAIN? WELL, YOU ARE NOT ALONE! THESE TWO PSALMS LOOK FOR GOD, THROUGH FAITH, WHEN IT'S MOST DIFFICULT. HOW?

YOU ARE NOT ALONE!

• By asking God questions (42:2,9). Talk to him and ask him what he is trying to teach you. In Psalm 43:2, the psalmist does ask 'why have you abandoned me?', 'why must I go on suffering?' and 'why am I so sad?'

• By asking for light and truth (43:3). It's worst when we are confused, stumbling around in darkness. Who was it who said he was light and truth? Look up John 8:12 and John 14:6. Remember that God demands honesty from us.

For any relationship to work, honesty is required. God is always truthful with us.

• By asking for help when you need it (42:6-8) – not afterwards! The writer is determined to look to the future: 'I will put my hope in God ... I will praise him.' Too often we try to do things in our own strength and then when we have tried everything and failed, seek God. Look for God's strength in *everything* that you do.

ACTION

• WRITE OUT PSALM 43:5 AND KEEP IT TO LOOK AT WHEN YOU ARE DISCOURAGED.

• CHECK OUT ROMANS 5:3,4. WHAT DOES IT TELL US ABOUT SUFFERING HERE?

CHECK OUT

PSALM 30

IT'S USUALLY THE DIFFICULT TIMES
THAT TEACH US MOST ABOUT GOD,
OTHERS AND OURSELVES.

• If you are in a rough patch now, look at verses 4 and 5. Problems attack your 'God-perspective' – they make you forget God and leave him out of the picture. But faith can exercise your 'God-perspective'! At the end of the problem God is there. In fact, looking back, you'll find that he was there all along.

• If you've come through a rocky time, remember that it's not just your own faith that pulled you through. It's God who supported you. He even gives us the faith! And that's worth saying 'thanks' for. Which is exactly what this psalm does.

Look at verse 6. Is this attitude right? Or is there a clue here to why God allowed the writer to suffer? What should our security be based on?

ACTION

• GET HOLD OF A CASSETTE OR CD OF NOEL RICHARDS SONG 'OUR CONFIDENCE IS IN THE LORD'. PLAY IT THROUGH AND PICTURE IN YOUR MIND THE PROBLEMS THAT CURRENTLY THREATEN OR WORRY YOU. AS YOU PICTURE THEM IN YOUR MIND LET THE WORDS OF THE SONG WASH OVER THE SITUATION AND BRING IT INTO PERSPECTIVE.

DAYZD 18

PSALM 51

I DOUBT WHETHER MOST OF US HAVE SINNED AS OBVIOUSLY AS DAVID (YOU CAN LOOK UP THE STORY IN 2 SAMUEL 11:2-5,14-17). BUT I AM SURE THAT ALL OF US HAVE SINNED AS DELIBERATELY AS HE DID. ALL SIN, ANY SIN, EFFECTIVELY WRENCHES US AWAY FROM GOD.

I remember a TV programme about a submarine half-flooded through bad navigation. New recruits were trapped in front. Rescuers were penned in at the rear. The water formed an impassable barrier in between. Rescue meant that one man must drown to clear the flooded compartment and bring the crew back together.

In Psalm 51, the psalmist, David recognises the law of cause and effect. The cause – he's sinned (vs 3-5). Sin is ultimately against God, not just his people (v 4). And sin is built into us (v 5). The effect is that the link with God is gone. The people of God may be endangered too (v 18), because our sin can lead others astray or destroy the unity of God's people.

ACTION

• WHEN WE KNOW THAT WE HAVE SINNED, WHAT IS OUR PART IN RESTORING THE LINK BETWEEN GOD AND US (VS 6,16,17)?

• WHAT IS GOD'S PART (VS 7,9,10)?

PSALM 32

HERE'S A FURTHER 'CAUSE AND EFFECT' PSALM. SIN BREAKS THE LINK BETWEEN GOD AND MAN, THEN CONFESSION RESTORES IT.

When David keeps quiet about his sin he goes on a 'downer' – discouragement, depression, apathy, even physical illness (vs 3,4)! But when he decides to talk it over with God (an act of will), he is again happy and forgiven (v 5). He gets protection (v 7), guidance (v 8), and joy (v 11). The cause is confession the effect is forgiveness.

Sin must lead to either punishment or mercy. Look up 1 John 1:8,9. God is in the confession-forgiveness-cleansing business. The measure of his investment is the cross of Jesus. Ask yourself 'What should my investment in the confession business be, today?'

SIN BREAKS THE LINK BETWEEN GOD AND MAN.

ACTION

• SPEND SOME TIME WITH GOD NOW, TELLING HIM ABOUT THE THINGS THAT YOU HAVE BEEN KEEPING TO YOURSELF. SOMETIMES THE BURDEN OF WHAT WE ARE CARRYING BECOMES SO GREAT AND WE HAVE TO OFF-LOAD IT ON TO SOMEONE. GOD IS THERE READY TO RECEIVE.

CHECK OUT

PSALM 103

CONFESSION IS PERSONAL, FOR OUR OWN SINS. IT'S ALSO CORPORATE, FOR THE SINS OF NATIONS. THIS WRITER IS PRAISING GOD FOR HIS PERSONAL DEALINGS WITH HIM. SO VERSES 2-5 ARE AN 'ACTION REPLAY' OF GOD'S GOODNESS TO THE INDIVIDUAL, FROM PAST SINS TO PRESENT BLESSINGS.

But praising God makes us look at his personality too; see verses 6-14. This section widens the picture: This is God's world; he's still got his hand on it; he deals with everyone with love and justice. This leads to our future benefit (v 17). Finally, verses 19-22 are a great shout of praise to God. They are a statement of fact (v 19) and a command to the writer's own soul (v 22). We're back to the personal again!

Take some time to:

• Praise God for something from the past.
• Praise for something in your future.
• Praise him for what he is like now.

ACTION

• IF YOU ARE QUITE ARTY, WHY NOT DRAW A CARTOON OF YOUR LIFE. START FROM WHEN YOU WERE A BABY (PAST), A DRAWING OF YOU NOW (PRESENT), AND A DRAWING OF WHAT YOU ARE GOING TO BE LIKE IN THE FUTURE! NEXT TO EACH DRAWING WRITE AN ITEM FOR PRAISE.

• IT IS QUITE HARD FOR US TO IMAGINE WHAT OUR FUTURE IS GOING TO BE LIKE – WILL I HAVE A GOOD JOB? WILL I HAVE A BIG CAR? WILL I BE MARRIED AND HAVE CHILDREN?! REMEMBER THAT WE ARE TOLD THAT, BECAUSE OF JESUS' DEATH AND RESURRECTION, OUR FUTURE HAS BEEN TAKEN CARE OF. SPEND SOME TIME THANKING GOD, THAT IN THE UNCERTAINTY OF OUR LIFE ON EARTH, IT IS A REAL JOY TO KNOW THAT OUR *REAL* FUTURE IS IN HIS HANDS.

CHECK OUT
PSALM 1

THE BIBLE CONTAINS SOME OF THE MOST BEAUTIFUL YET HARD-HITTING LANGUAGE EVER WRITTEN. THE PSALMS ESPECIALLY ARE THUMB-NAIL SKETCHES OF LIFE AS IT REALLY IS. POETIC THEY MAY BE, BUT 'WET' THEY ARE NOT!

Psalm 1 is direct and realistic. It's an 'hour-glass' shape; one part (vs 1-3) the exact reverse of the next (vs 4-6). Notice how verse 4 contrasts with verse 3, verse 5 with verse 2, verse 6 with verse 1. The two parts describe two paths, leading to two destinations. The happiness and success of the righteous (vs 1-3) are sharply etched against the barrenness and destruction of evil men (vs 4-6). Think about the difference between a firmly-rooted tree (v 3) and a piece of straw (v 4). Which would you rather be when the wind blows?

LIFE AS IT REALLY IS !

Notice that obedience to God isn't a deadly duty (though it does involve some hard work). But is actually enjoyable (v 2).

Which most accurately describes your reaction to this psalm?

• I agree. Those who follow God have a happier life than those who don't.
• I'm a bit puzzled. Often the 'wicked' seem to have an easier time of it.
• I think the 'righteous' do get their reward but not until heaven.

Talk to God about the one you've ticked; ask him to show you the truth.

ACTION

• TAKE SOME TIME TO THINK ABOUT YOUR OWN LIFE. WOULD YOU DESCRIBE YOUR LIFE LIKE A TREE THAT GROWS BESIDE A STREAM? IF NOT, IN WHAT WAYS DO YOU THINK YOUR LIFE COULD BE MORE LIKE THE PSALMIST'S DESCRIPTION (VS 1,2)?

DAY-Z-D 22

PROVERBS 9

WISDOM VERSUS STUPIDITY. BUT THE STAKES ARE HIGHER THAN THAT: IT'S LIFE VERSUS DEATH. OBEYING AND KNOWING GOD MEANS LIFE. CONCEIT, EVIL AND STUPIDITY MEANS DEATH.

'Wisdom' and 'Stupidity' both throw a party. It is reassuring that 'Wisdom' invites ordinary, common, simple, even ignorant people. People like us. It is frightening that 'Stupidity' invites the same people. People like us! Two parties, two destinations. Which one are you going to choose?

Check out Proverbs 9 before answering these questions:

• 'Wisdom's' preparations for the feast are carefully described (vs 1,2). Has 'Stupidity' got any real 'goodies' to offer (vs 13-18)?

• Where do we have to begin if we want wisdom (v 10)?

• Read verses 7-9 again. How do you react if a more mature Christian tells you that you're wrong?

• Describe your idea of a wise person.

• LISTEN TO 'HOLD ON', *IT'S A SMALL WORLD, SPRING HARVEST 1995.*

CHECK OUT
AMOS 1:3-2:8

THIS PASSAGE DESCRIBES WHAT GOD PUNISHES. IN ONE WORD, SIN. GOD NEVER ACTS HASTILY OR WITHOUT CAUSE. THESE ARE THE SINS OF WHOLE NATIONS, REPEATED AGAIN AND AGAIN (VS 3,6,9,11,13, ETC) IN DEFIANCE OF GOD'S LAW.

In the middle of the word 'SIN' is 'I'. In the middle of the sins of nations are my sins. In the eighth century before Christ, God outlines the sins of Israel's neighbours (1:3–2:3). List them in your own words.

They are the sins of the twentieth century AD too: cruelty, oppression, faithlessness, treachery, anger and grudges, intimidation, irreverence, disobedience and rebellion.

But worse, God must also outline the sins of his chosen people, Israel and Judah (2:4-8). Nowadays, that means you and me. Are we Christians any different from the world around us? If not, God will have to punish us too.

Am I or is my church guilty of any of these sins:
• Oppressing or neglecting the poor (vs 6,7a)?
• Treating people as things (v 7b)?
• Enjoying prosperity at the expense of others (v 8)?

Am I or is my church doing anything actively to fight these sins in the world?

ACTION

• PRAY THAT GOD WILL MAKE YOU ANGRY ABOUT THE SINS THAT MAKE HIM ANGRY.

• PICK OUT ONE COUNTRY WHICH YOU HAVE HEARD ABOUT, EITHER ON TELEVISION OR READ ABOUT IN A NEWSPAPER, WHICH IS FACING CRUELTY, OPPRESSION, TREACHERY ANGER AND GRUDGES. OVER THE NEXT THREE MONTHS (OR AS LONG AS YOU CAN MANAGE TO DO IT FOR!) PRAY FOR THE NEEDS OF THE PEOPLE OF THAT COUNTRY. KEEP A NOTE OF THE THINGS WHICH ANGER OR HURT YOU FROM WHAT YOU HAVE HEARD OR READ. GIVE THESE TO GOD. KEEP A NOTE OF ALL THE GOOD THINGS WHICH HAVE HAPPENED IN THAT COUNTRY OVER THE LAST FEW MONTHS. GIVE THANKS TO GOD FOR THEM.

PSALM 15

THESE DAYS EVERYONE IS LOOKING FOR ALL THE RIGHT THINGS IN ALL THE WRONG PLACES. MANY LOOK FOR SECURITY IN SEX, MONEY, CARS, A JOB, A CD SYSTEM OR IN A BOY/GIRLFRIEND. HERE GOD SAYS CLEARLY HOW TO ATTAIN REAL SECURITY (V 5B). BEING RIGHT WITH HIM DOESN'T JUST MEAN NOT DOING WRONG (V 3); BUT TAKING ACTION THAT IS RIGHT (VS 2,4B,5). GOD'S KIND OF PERSON HAS INTEGRITY, HONESTY, REAL GUTS TO STAND UP FOR WHAT'S RIGHT AND REJECT WHAT'S WRONG. ABOVE ALL, HE OR SHE IS OBEDIENT. GOD NOTICES. SO DOES THE WORLD.

THESE DAYS
EVERYONE IS LOOKING FOR
ALL THE RIGHT THINGS IN ALL
THE WRONG PLACES.

Compare verse 4a to Jesus' words in Matthew 5:43-45. What attitude should a Christian have to those who do wrong?

Look at v 4b. Think about the promises you have made to God. Are you prepared to keep them no matter what the cost? Pray that God will help you worship him and him alone.

ACTION

• DO YOU FIND IT HARD NOT TO PUT A GIRLFRIEND/BOYFRIEND RELATIONSHIP BEFORE GOD? PRAY FOR GOD'S HELP IN THIS SITUATION.

• OVER THE NEXT MONTH SPEND SOME TIME READING *IT'S ALWAYS ON MY MIND* BY J.JOHN OR *SET FREE* BY JOHN WHITE, PUBLISHED BY EAGLE.

JOB 1

EVEN THOUGH THE CHRISTIAN LIFE ISN'T A COMPLETE BED OF ROSES IT IS FANTASTIC, EXCITING AND BEAUTIFUL. BUT IN EVERY BED OF ROSES THERE ARE ALSO THORNS. YOU CAN'T HAVE ONE WITHOUT THE OTHER. LOOK UP JOHN 17:15. JESUS KNEW WHAT HE WAS PRAYING ABOUT; THE FACT IS, THE RIGHTEOUS DO SUFFER.

Read Job 1 and then look at the following questions and think through the answers:

1. Name Job's good qualities.

2. Who causes all the havoc?

3. Who allows it all?

4. What's really being tested (vs 9-11)?

5. Where does God draw the line (see 2:4-6)?

6. What is Job's reaction (1:20,21,2:9,10)?

Tick the statements you believe to be true and check your answers against the story of Job:

• God's people always have their problems solved quickly.
• Suffering tests our faith in God.
• We only suffer when we have disobeyed God.
• God has no power to stop us suffering.
• When we are miserable, we shouldn't show it.
• Suffering should not destroy our belief in God.
• God will not let us suffer more than we can bear.

ACTION

• LISTEN TO 'I WILL WAIT', *IT'S A SMALL WORLD, SPRING HARVEST PRAISE MIX 1995.* PRAY THAT GOD WILL HELP YOU TO BE PATIENT IN DIFFICULT TIMES.

• ALTERNATIVELY READ THROUGH THE LYRICS AND SPEND SOME TIME MEDITATING ON THEM:

I WILL WAIT FOR YOUR PEACE TO COME TO ME
I WILL WAIT FOR YOUR PEACE TO COME TO ME
AND I'LL SING IN THE DARKNESS
AND I'LL WAIT WITHOUT FEAR
AND I'LL SING IN THE DARKNESS
AND I'LL WAIT WITHOUT FEAR.

DAY'Z'D 26

PSALM 73

GOD'S PLAN FOR CHRISTIANS ALLOWS SUFFERING,
PAIN, PERSECUTION. BUT IT DOESN'T ALLOW
CHRISTIANS TO PERISH. 'PERISHING' HERE
(V 27) DOESN'T MEAN JUST DYING. WE WILL
ALL DIE. JESUS SAID WE ARE TO FEAR GOD
'WHO CAN DESTROY BOTH BODY AND
SOUL IN HELL' (MATTHEW 10:28).
THAT IS THE BOTTOM LINE. THE
RIGHTEOUS MAY SUFFER, BUT
THE WICKED PERISH.

THE BOTTOM LINE.

Perhaps you have looked at
your non-Christian friends
and secretly wished you
weren't a Christian and
could do 'that', whatever
'that' is. You might join in
and sin, and forget God. But
what good to gain 'security'
on earth and lose heaven?

Read Psalm 73 again.

Describe in your own words the basic
problem the psalm-writer was struggling with
(vs 2,3,12,13).

What was it that made him suddenly see
things differently (vs 16,17)?

ACTION

• LOOK BACK AT PAGE 27 AT THE ANSWER YOU TICKED
ON PSALM 1. HAS TODAY'S PSALM MADE THIS CLEARER
TO YOU?

• START TO KEEP A RECORD OF ALL THE VERSES THAT
YOU DISCOVER WHILST USING *DAYZD*, WHICH YOU FIND
PARTICULARLY ENCOURAGING. YOU COULD START A
JOURNAL, NOT ONLY WRITING DOWN THE VERSE BUT
THE REASON WHY YOU FOUND IT ENCOURAGING
(PERHAPS EVEN ADDING A DATE).

GENESIS 12:1-9

GOD TAKES AND USES ORDINARY, INSIGNIFICANT PEOPLE.

I AM GRATEFUL GOD TAKES AND USES ORDINARY, INSIGNIFICANT PEOPLE. UNLIKELY PEOPLE. LOOK AT ABRAM. SEVENTY-FIVE YEARS OLD AND NOT GETTING ANY YOUNGER! CHOSEN BY GOD, AND SENT OFF TO 'DESTINATION UNCONFIRMED', LEAVING BEHIND HOME, RELATIVES, FRIENDS AND POSSESSIONS! IN CHOOSING THE ONE ORDINARY PERSON, GOD CHOSE A WHOLE PEOPLE (V 2). THERE WERE FOUR FACTORS AT WORK:

1. God's prompting: his call, based on his initiative.
2. God's purpose: a clear, strong plan of action.
3. God's promise: 'I will ... I will ...'.
4. God's enabling power. Never go it alone, go it with God.

God works the same way today. If he promises, he provides.

• Does God expect people to follow his call all on their own? Read verses 4 and 5.

• Check out Genesis 17:4,5. Why do you think Abram was given a new name?

ACTION

• IS GOD CALLING YOU TO BE MORE INVOLVED IN YOUR CHURCH/YOUTH GROUP? WHY NOT HAVE A CHAT TO YOUR MINISTER OR YOUTH LEADER TO SEE IF THERE ARE WAYS IN WHICH YOUR GIFTS CAN BE USED.

DAYZD 28

CHECK OUT

EXODUS 15:1-18

GOD DOESN'T CHOOSE A PEOPLE TO LOSE A PEOPLE. WHAT HE STARTS, HE FINISHES. ABRAHAM'S DESCENDANTS BECAME SLAVES IN EGYPT, WHERE THEY HAD GONE TO ESCAPE FAMINE. SO WHAT WAS GOING TO HAPPEN TO THE PROMISED LAND GOD HAD SENT ABRAHAM TO?

This song of victory tells us what did happen. God chose Moses to bring his people out of Egypt. By a miracle he helped them escape from the Egyptian army that followed them (the story is in Exodus 14:15,16,26,27).

No one closes God's open doors. Nothing stops God – not nature (vs 11,12), not man (vs 14,15). When God saves his chosen people he does it completely.

ACTION

• LOOK AT VERSE 5 AND THINK ABOUT WHAT GOD CAN DO TO THE 'ENEMIES' YOU ARE FACED WITH. WHAT ARE YOU A 'SLAVE' TO - BEING CYNICAL? FALLING IN LOVE WITH THE WRONG PEOPLE? JEALOUSY? FOOD? NAME YOUR 'ENEMY' AND PRAY FOR GOD'S VICTORY OVER IT.

• READ *TAMING THE LION*, BY CATHIE BARTLAM, SCRIPTURE UNION. THIS EXCELLENT STORY TAKES THE READER THROUGH THE LIFE OF MEL, SOMEONE WHO IS STRUGGLING WITH AN EATING DISORDER.

• QUOTE: IF GOD IS FOR US, WHO CAN BE AGAINST US? ROMANS 8:31.

CHECK OUT
PSALM 136

OUR PSALM TODAY SHOULD REALLY BE SUNG AND NOT JUST READ! THERE'S A BUILT-IN BEAT TO THIS ONE, HAMMERING HOME THE TRUTH THAT 'HIS LOVE IS ETERNAL'. IN PUBLIC WORSHIP PROBABLY ONE GROUP SANG THE VERSE LINES, AND ANOTHER THE CHORUS. SO IT WOULD REALLY SWING BACKWARDS AND FORWARDS!

Why does the psalmist keep coming back to God's love? Some of the verses are pretty heavy: killing and drowning all over the place! I think it's because God does act in the whole of human history. He won't turn his back on the dirty side of history; his love for his people means getting involved in anything that happens to them. He acts in history because it's 'his story'; he created it (vs 4-9) and he'll go to great lengths to keep his people safe and pure.

ACTION

• WRITE YOUR OWN VERSION OF PSALM 136 TELLING THE STORY OF WHAT GOD HAS DONE FOR YOU.

• TRY AND SET THIS PSALM TO MUSIC YOURSELF - OR EVEN TRY AND SING IT TO THE TUNE OF A FAVOURITE SONG.

DAYZD 30

PSALM 124

HOW EASY IT IS FOR US TO FORGET THE GOOD TIMES WHEN LIFE ISN'T SO GREAT. HOW MANY TIMES DO YOU CATCH YOURSELF THINKING 'MY LIFE IS SO HARD. WHY GOD, DO YOU MAKE ME GO THROUGH THIS WHEN LIFE FOR (ADD NAME OF APPROPRIATE PERSON) IS SO EASY?' AND WHY IS IT THAT IT ALWAYS SEEMS EVERYONE ELSE IN THE WORLD IS HAVING AN EASY RIDE IN LIFE?

WHY GOD, DO YOU MAKE ME GO THROUGH THIS ?

Read Psalm 124. God's people ought to say 'What if ...' (v 1) more often! We'll never be sure how many disasters God keeps us from. Here the psalmist reminds God's people of a scrape that God had got them out of – and praise the Lord that he did (vs 1-5)! How quickly we forget the good things God has done for us!

Look back on your own life. Can you see times when God has intervened in a bad situation for you? Pray to God that he may give you the ability to trust him to do the same in the present and the future.

ACTION

• IF YOU HAVE STARTED TO KEEP A JOURNAL OF ALL THE VERSES YOU HAVE FOUND ENCOURAGING, READ THROUGH THIS PSALM AGAIN AND SEE IF THERE IS ONE HERE WHICH YOU WOULD LIKE TO ADD TO YOUR LIST. AGAIN, WRITE NEXT TO IT THE REASONS WHY YOU WERE ENCOURAGED BY IT AND KEEP IT SAFE FOR THE DAYS WHEN YOU NEED A LITTLE ENCOURAGEMENT.

PSALM 87

THERE'S A KIND OF SPIRITUAL LOGIC WORKING HERE. IT GOES LIKE THIS: ISRAEL IS THE CENTRE OF GOD'S LOVE, JERUSALEM IS THE CENTRE OF ISRAEL, THEREFORE JERUSALEM IS THE CENTRE OF GOD'S LOVE. THE ISRAELITES LOVED JERUSALEM PASSIONATELY - LOOK AT PSALM 137:5,6!

We still use 'Jerusalem' or 'Zion' (the hill it was built on) as a word for heaven. But as 'Israel' was widened by Jesus Christ's coming and now means all of God's people, not just the Jews; so 'Jerusalem' too is widened. God has started the building of a new Jerusalem (Revelation 21:1-4) that will only be completed when Jesus Christ comes again. Jerusalem is where God rules, and that can start with you and me! We are looking right ahead, to the time when even enemies will be united in Christ. Philistia, Tyre and Ethiopia were age-old enemies of Israel. The Israelites tended to think that because God had chosen them, they were better than all the other nations. But God says here that he has chosen them in order to bring other nations to himself (vs 4,5).

ACTION

• LOOK UP MATTHEW 28:19,20 AND GALATIANS 3:28. NOW ANSWER THESE QUESTIONS HONESTLY:

WHAT IS MY ATTITIUDE TO THOSE WHO DON'T KNOW GOD?

☐ I DISAPPROVE OF WHAT THEY DO AND KEEP AWAY FROM THEM.
☐ I TRY TO TELL THEM THE GOOD NEWS ABOUT JESUS.
☐ I THANK GOD I'M NOT WICKED LIKE THEM.

WHAT IS MY ATTITUDE TO PEOPLE FROM OTHER RACES OR BACKGROUNDS?

☐ I THINK THEY SHOULD STAY WITH THEIR OWN KIND.
☐ I'M A LITTLE FRIGHTENED OF THEM.
☐ I TRY TO MAKE FRIENDS WITH THEM.

WHAT DO YOU THINK YOUR ATTITUDE TO 'OUTSIDERS' *SHOULD* BE?

DEUTERONOMY 17:14-20

EVER COME ACROSS 'WORM THEOLOGY'? THAT'S THE IDEA THAT IN GOD'S EYES YOU ARE MISERABLE, USELESS - REALLY JUST A WORM. LIKE EVERY LIE OF SATAN, IT'S HALF TRUE. LEFT TO OURSELVES, WE ARE LIKE THAT. BUT GOD DIDN'T LEAVE US TO OURSELVES; HE MADE US HIS SONS AND DAUGHTERS. NOT ONLY THAT, BUT HE IS ALSO MAKING US INTO PEOPLE FIT TO RULE WITH HIM (REVELATION 3:21). IN GOD'S EYES, WE ARE PRINCES AND PRINCESSES!

'WORM THEOLOGY'?

More than 1,000 years before Jesus, God set out the requirements for a king of his chosen people. We can use them to examine how well we match up to the kingship God's given us:

1. Being the person of God's choice (v 15a). Am I the kind of person God wants me to be?
2. Being part of God's people (v 15b). Am I really part of my local church?
3. Not relying on anything other than God (v 16). Is my security based on something other than God?
4. Dedication to God (v 17). What distracts me from God?
5. Following God's instructions (vs 18,19). What do I believe God has been saying to me recently? Have I done it?

ACTION

QUOTE: 'GOD KNOWS HOW TO RIDE THE LAME HORSE AND CARVE THE ROTTEN WOOD'.
MARTIN LUTHER

CHECK OUT

PSALM 101

EVER SINCE THE MAGNA CARTA IN 1215, THE KINGS OF THIS COUNTRY HAVE BEEN ANSWERABLE TO THE LAW. THE KING OR QUEEN IS A PERSON OF AUTHORITY, BUT ALSO A PERSON UNDER AUTHORITY – THE AUTHORITY OF RIGHT AND WRONG. THE QUEEN CAN'T JUST DO WHAT SHE FEELS LIKE – THAT WOULD MAKE HER A TYRANT OR A DICTATOR! GOD'S 'KINGS AND QUEENS' ARE THE SAME: PEOPLE OF AUTHORITY, BUT UNDER THE AUTHORITY OF GOD.

Read Psalm 101. Commitment to worship God is an act of the will. That's why there are a lot of 'I will's' in this psalm.

• List all the promises the psalmist makes here.

• Read verse I again. In the *Good News* translation it reads 'My song is about loyalty and justice'. Write down what loyalty means to you.

• Is there a situation in which God is asking you to be loyal – to him or to his people?

• Now write down what 'justice' means to you.

• Is there anyone you have been unjust to? Or a way in which you could help to make the world you live in more just?

ACTION

• LISTEN TO 'GOD OF CREATION WE PRAISE YOU', *SMALL WORLD, SPRING HARVEST 1995.*

DAYZD 34

2 CHRONICLES 7:11-22

LIKE CHURCH BUILDINGS OF TODAY, THE TEMPLE IN JERUSALEM WAS THE CENTRE OF RELIGIOUS LIFE FOR GOD'S PEOPLE. BUT THE TEMPLE WAS ONLY A SYMBOL; WHAT MATTERED WAS THE ATTITUDE OF THE PEOPLE WHO WENT THERE. THE TEMPLE ITSELF COULD NOT PROTECT ANYONE FROM GOD'S JUDGMENT IF THEY DISOBEYED HIM!

Here God outlines the task of the temple. It is to be a place of sacrifice, where people offer valuable gifts to God (v 12). It's the place where prayers are made, not only individual, but the prayers of nations too (v 15). It's a place of repentance, where forgiveness is available (v 14). It's somewhere set aside for God where he is worshipped (v 16a). It's a place of protection and refuge (v 16b). It is to be a great place that reflects God's great (see chapter 2 verse 5).

The temple in Jerusalem was destroyed in 70 AD and never rebuilt. Where's the main centre of God's love today? Amazingly, nowadays the temple is a living one – it's you and me! (1 Peter 2:5).

THINK ABOUT HOW YOU OR YOUR CHURCH CAN CARRY ON THE TASK OF THE TEMPLE IN THESE AREAS:
• OFFERING GIFTS TO GOD (SEE ROMANS 12:1).
• HELPING PEOPLE TO PRAY.
• WORSHIPPING GOD.
• HELPING PEOPLE TO FIND FORGIVENESS.
• PROTECTING PEOPLE FROM HARM.
• REFLECTING THE BEAUTY OF GOD.

DAYZD 35

PSALM 84

IN AUSTRALIA THERE IS A PHRASE SIMILAR TO THE ENGLISH PHRASE 'HOME AND DRY', EXCEPT IN AUSTRALIA WHERE IT IS OFTEN HOT AND DRY THE PHRASE USED IS 'HOME AND HOSED'. PSALM 84 MIGHT WELL HAVE BEEN WRITTEN AS A BURST OF DELIGHT BY A WEARY PILGRIM ON REACHING THE TEMPLE IN JERUSALEM. THERE'S A SENSE OF FULFILLED LONGING, OF COMING HOME. HEADING TOWARDS THE TEMPLE, AFTER TRUDGING THROUGH DIFFICULT AND DRY PLACES LIKE THE DESERT VALLEY OF BACA, MAKES EVEN THE PROBLEMS SEEM WORTHWHILE. GOD'S PEOPLE DON'T AVOID LIFE'S PROBLEMS, THEY GET STRETCHED THROUGH THEM.

Yet if you look carefully you can't help realising that it's not strictly the temple that the psalmist loves. It's the presence of God and all that he brings: happiness, strength, kindness and honour, protection and good gifts. The writer's real love is for God, who is found in his temple.

Have you really got an intense love for God? If not, ask him to grow it in you. If you're spending time seeking him in these studies, the seeds are already there!

ACTION

• WITH YOUR EYES CLOSED, TRY TO IMAGINE THAT YOU ARE ON A LONG JOURNEY, HAVING TO TRUDGE THROUGH DIFFICULT AND DRY PLACES. THE SUN IS HOT AND YOU ARE REALLY SWEATY AND THIRSTY. BUT WAIT, WHAT'S THAT? A HUGE AND COOL FRESH-WATER POOL LAYS IN FRONT OF YOU – HALLELUJAH! REFRESHMENT AT LAST! THE CHRISTIAN LIFE IS A JOURNEY, AND SOMETIMES WE FEEL IN DESPERATE NEED OF SPIRITUAL REFRESHMENT. TAKE SOME TIME NOW TO ASK GOD TO REFRESH YOU SO THAT YOU CAN CONTINUE IN YOUR JOURNEY WITH HIM.

• HAVE YOU EVER SEEN A POT PLANT WHICH HAS BEEN LEFT FOR A LONG TIME WITHOUT WATER? EVEN WHEN YOU DO REMEMBER TO GIVE IT A DRINK, IT HAS BECOME SO DRY THAT IT IS UNABLE TO HOLD THE VERY THING WHICH IS GOING TO REVIVE IT. THE ONLY WAY TO SAVE IT IS TO SOAK THE PLANT IN A BUCKET OF COOL WATER, SO THAT IT HAS A CONSTANT SUPPLY. IT IS THE SAME FOR US. WE NEED TO SPEND REGULAR TIME WITH GOD, EG THROUGH PRAYER AND READING THE BIBLE, SO THAT WE DO NOT BECOME 'SPIRITUALLY DRY'. ARE YOU FEELING WELL-WATERED AT THE MOMENT?

PSALM 119:1-24

LIFE WITHOUT RULES IS CHAOS.

LIFE WITHOUT RULES IS CHAOS. YOU COULDN'T RIDE SAFELY IN BUSES IF ROAD RULES WERE IGNORED. YOU COULDN'T MAKE DECENT CAKES IF COOKING RULES WERE THROWN OUT. YOU COULDN'T ENJOY PLAYING OR WINNING FOOTBALL IF THE RULES WERE ABANDONED. REAL FREEDOM COMES WHEN WE OBEY THE RULES.

This writer sees that sticking with God's rules isn't just a duty, it's the way to happiness (vs 1,2). That's why verse 5 sounds eager, excited, longing to aim at the goal of obedience.

What comes over here is the three 'L's:
• learning the rules.
• loving the rules.
• living the rules.

Think of at least two ways in which you can learn God's rules:

ACTION

• ASK GOD TO HELP YOU LOVE HIS RULES AND LIVE BY THEM.

HOSEA 11:1-10

GOD
CHOSE ISRAEL
AS HIS SPECIAL PEOPLE,
AND RESCUED THEM FROM BEING
SLAVES IN EGYPT. BUT VERSE 2
CONTINUES THE STORY: IN SPITE OF ALL THIS, THE
ISRAELITES REBELLED AGAINST GOD AGAIN AND AGAIN.
VERSES 3-10 SHOW US HOW GOD FELT ABOUT IT.

You'd expect a prophet like Hosea to reveal the very heartbeat of God. Prophets are special people with ears tuned to God, and mouths that pass on the message faithfully. That's what happens here. Hosea hears and passes on the strong, compassionate, aching love of God for his children.

Teenagers often hurt their parents by rebelling against them. When God's children do the same, three things happen. First, we grieve God to the depth of his heart – he feels the anguish of our rebellion. Second, we lose ourselves, because we can only find our real self in God. Third, we face the consequences just as Israel did (vs 5-7).

Yet like a loving parent, God is willing to welcome the wayward child back. Does this remind you of a well-known story in the New Testament? (Check out Luke 15:11 onwards!).

ACTION

• THINK ABOUT THE WAYS IN WHICH YOU HAVE REBELLED AGAINST GOD. WHAT IDOLS DO YOU WORSHIP IN PREFERENCE TO GOD. WHY DO YOU CHOOSE THEM INSTEAD OF GOD?

• READ VERSES 3B,4 AND MEDITATE ON THEM. IF YOU FEEL IT IS APPROPRIATE, ASK GOD TO FORGIVE YOU FOR TURNING YOUR BACK ON HIM.

PSALM 50

IT'S GOOD THAT GOD WON'T JUST SIT BACK AND LET US POTTER ON UP SOME DEAD-END ALLEY! SOMETIMES, LIKE HERE, HE NEEDS TO GIVE A VERY SHARP AND TIMELY REMINDER OF THE REAL ROUTE.

GOD WON'T JUST SIT BACK !

Just like us, the people of Israel had a tendency to get side-tracked. Some thought that giving sacrifices was the way to God (vs 8-13). We don't kill animals today to earn God's favour. But instead of 'bulls and goats' read 'money in the offering plate' or whatever sacrifices you're most proud of ...

Others were trying to impress God by making lots of rules for themselves (v 16). We're still very good at that! Others had wandered deep into sin (vs 17-20).

All these dead ends are still around! The direction God wants us to give us is simpler. Real sacrifice means that we see our need of help (v 15), we are thankful and we are obedient (vs 14,23).

ACTION

• TIME FOR HONESTY! LIST THE THINGS YOU DO BECAUSE YOU HOPE THEY'LL IMPRESS GOD/OTHER CHRISTIANS:

• NOW SPEND SOME TIME IN PRAYER ASKING HIM TO SHOW YOU WHAT HE REALLY WANTS FROM YOU.

CHECK OUT

AMOS 5:10-27

ALTHOUGH GOD IS INCREDIBLY PATIENT WITH US, THERE COMES A TIME WHEN, TO BE TRUE TO HIMSELF, HE MUST SAY 'ENOUGH IS ENOUGH'. AND THAT'S WHAT HE IS SAYING HERE THROUGH HIS SERVANT AMOS. IF GOD'S PEOPLE WON'T OBEY HIS COMMANDS, THEN THEY MUST FACE THE CONSEQUENCES – EXILE FROM THE PLACE OF GOD'S BLESSING (VS 26,27). THE PROMISED LAND WILL BE TAKEN AWAY.

Another promise will be turned on its head. The Day of the Lord (vs 18-20) was a time the Israelites hoped for, when the other nations, who disobeyed God, would be judged and condemned. But Amos says it's Israel itself that will be condemned for its disobedience!

Look at verses 18 and 21 again. It's not wrong to hope for God's great day – for Christians that means the day when Jesus will return to rule the world. It's not wrong to hold big religious festivals either (v 21)! But the point is that neither of these on their own can guarantee that you're doing what God wants. Look at verse 24 to find out what that is.

How important are justice and righteousness to you? Have you ever spoken out on behalf of someone who was being unfairly treated?

ACTION

• 'JUSTICE IS TRUTH IN ACTION.' BENJAMIN DISRAELI.

• WATCH THE NEWS. IMAGINE HOW EACH NEWS ITEM WOULD BE DIFFERENT IF JUSTICE AND RIGHTEOUSNESS WERE TO OCCUR THROUGH THEM. PRAY FOR JUSTICE AND RIGHTEOUSNESS TO ENTER INTO THESE SITUATIONS.

• IF YOU ARE INTERESTED IN GETTING INVOLVED WITH CAMPAIGNING FOR JUSTICE AND HUMAN RIGHTS, CONTACT JUBILEE CAMPAIGN OR CHRISTIAN SOLIDARITY INTERNATIONAL FOR MORE INFORMATION.

DAYZD 40

PSALM 79

IT'S EASY TO FORGET THAT EVEN THOSE WHO DON'T KNOW GOD LIVE, BREATH AND EXIST ONLY BECAUSE GOD WITHHOLDS HIS JUDGMENT. CHECK OUT 2 PETER 3:7-9. GOD IS PATIENT WITH THE WORLD BECAUSE HE DOESN'T WANT ANYONE TO PERISH, TO BE LEFT WITHOUT HOPE.

When God's judgment does fall on a nation, it's an awesome thing. It happened to Israel, just as Amos and the other prophets warned that it would. The nation would not obey God, so they were attacked and almost destroyed by other nations. This psalm describes the devastation that was left.

Look at our nation now. It may seem bad, but what would happen if God judged us instead of giving us time to repent? What if this psalm described the invaded and devastated country where you live?

ACTION

• ASK GOD WHAT PLEASES OR PAINS HIM ABOUT THE COUNTRY WHERE YOU LIVE. TO START YOU THINKING, LOOK AT THE SINS AMOS DESCRIBED IN AMOS 5:10-13 (VS 10-13). IN OUR WORLD TODAY, ARE WE GUILTY OF DENYING JUSTICE TO THE POOR AND POWERLESS? TREATING WOMEN AS SEX OBJECTS? MISTREATING RACIAL MINORITIES OR THE DISABLED? THESE ARE THE KIND OF SINS FOR WHICH ISRAEL WAS JUDGED.

THIS STORY OCCURS AFTER ONE OF GOD'S GREAT JUDGMENTS ON ISRAEL. THE ISRAELITIES, GOD'S PEOPLE, HAVE BEEN SEVERELY OPPRESSED BY THE BABYLONIAN EMPIRE FOR YEARS. EZRA WRITES FOR THE TIME OF NEW BEGINNINGS. BABYLON HAS BEEN OVERTHROWN BY CYRUS OF PERSIA, AND AN EASIER TIME IS AHEAD. GOD'S PEOPLE ARE RETURNING TO THEIR COUNTRY AND THEIR FATHER.

The temple, symbol of the only God, and of the unity of his people, is to be rebuilt. The people themselves are called back together to the holy city of Jerusalem. Once again, sacrifice is to be made to the only true God. The judgment ends with a return to God, a reunion with one another, and a recommitment to a life of sacrifice to God.

ACTION

• IS THERE ANY WAY IN WHICH YOU'VE BEEN RUNNING AWAY FROM GOD? COME BACK TO HIM NOW - GIVING HIM THE PLACES WHERE YOU FEEL YOU HAVE FAILED. REMEMBER THAT GOD CAN REDEEM THESE PLACES OF APPARENT FAILURE - TURNING THEM INTO SOMETHING GOOD. READ ROMANS 8:28.

DAYZD 42

OVER THE NEXT TWO DAYS WE ARE GOING TO BE LOOKING AT WORSHIP THROUGH THE EYES OF THE EVANGELIST AND AUTHOR J.JOHN. EXAMINING PSALM 148 AND TALKING ABOUT HIS EXPERIENCE OF WORSHIP, J.JOHN TAKES US THROUGH THE SUBJECT OF CREATION PRAISE.

CHECK OUT PSALM 148

'Praise the Lord. Praise the Lord from the heavens. Praise him in the heights above ...' this psalm is incredible: it seems to suggest that the whole of creation was made to praise God. Instead of looking at singing, dancing and rejoicing in God's presence as something of little value, the Bible tells us that it is the very thing we were made for.

Have a quick think about some of the reasons your friends and contemporaries would say why they were made: to be successful, to have as much pleasure as they possibly can, to be fulfilled. What is the purpose of life? Around 300 years ago the Westminster Catechism said this: 'What is the chief end of man? Man's chief end is to glorify God and enjoy him for ever.'

Worship is the primary activity of the whole world. It requires no other justification beyond itself. God is to be praised, from the highest Heavens to the four corners of the earth. In fact when we do come together to celebrate God, we join not only with thousands of other voices but all the praises of heaven. Verse 2 says, 'praise him all his angels, praise him, all his heavenly host.'

The angels are praising constantly. In fact most of the pictures we have of heaven are not just of angels but multitudes of people. Revelation 7 verse 9 says there

are 'more than the eye can count' praising God. For those who have been to a worship event like Soul Survivor, you will know that you are part of something bigger, but it is not limited only to those events, it involves all God's people all around the world and in heaven. It is about a foretaste of heaven. So really it's not a worship leader who leads worship, it's not even the angels but it's the Spirit, because the Holy Spirit is the one who leads us into the presence of God.

'Praise him sun and moon. Praise him you shining stars ... Praise the Lord from the earth, you great creatures and all ocean depths, lightening and hail ... mountains and hills ... animals and cattle.'

But it's not only heaven which is constantly praising, it's the whole earth. In our arrogance we think that humans are the focus for the world; we have misused creation to our own ends. That seems to be the root of the dreadful waste of the environment, the treatment of the planet which, let's face it, we are all guilty of to some extent .

This psalm tells us that creation is not here for us; it is here for God. In fact

DAYZD 43 & 44

creation, sun and moon, stars and planets, whales, lions, tigers, trees and mountains were all made to praise God.

The main point is this, that the whole of creation was made for God, by God, to be directed to God in praise.

Our job as humans is to give voice to the praise of creation. We must as verse 13 says, 'Let them praise the Lord ...'.

In our celebration we not only join with the whole of God's people on earth and heaven but all creation. But hold on, in our celebration we are also aware that things aren't as they should be, in the creation, in the world and in ourselves. In Romans 8:18-27 the apostle Paul talks about the groaning of creation and the groaning of the children of God.

Why? Because the Spirit is drawing us into the future, when all things will truly worship God; but until then we live in a fallen world.

To put it starkly, if there is no sense that things should not be the way they are in the world, in creation and in our lives during worship, then the Spirit is not at work.

The Spirit brings dissatisfaction to us about the way things are.

Paul says that the Spirit causes us to groan with the pain of childbirth. Now I've never given birth but my wife tells me it's the most painful thing she has experienced.

Celebration in God's presence isn't a painless thing, and it certainly is not an escapist thing. Through intimacy with God and each other we are made aware of the fact that we are not yet in heaven, that creation cannot praise God properly because of our sin (which also prevents us from worshipping God fully) and we can't really worship God without the company of those we really love who do not love and adore Jesus.

Coming together in celebration fills us with new determination not only to live lives which worship God in every part, but to be those through whom all creation, friends, family and everyone we meet can come to worship God. From celebrations we are sent into the world to be God's agents of worship to call the whole world to proclaim God, to voice creation's praise.

J.John lives in Nottingham with his wife Killy, and sons Michael, Simeon and Ben. Well known as an evangelist, John is also involved with the work of Soul Survivor.

If you would like to know more about Soul Survivor youth events/publications write to Soul Survivor, 37 Quickley Lane, Chorleywood, Herts, WD3 5AE.

1.
• Check out Romans 8:20-22. What makes creation 'groan' instead of praise?

• How is God planning to make his world full of praise again? Check out Ephesians 1:10. If you would like to look at how this can happen read DAYZD: Evangelism.

2.
• It is easy for us to praise God when things are going well, but what about the times when life isn't that great. If you are going through a tough time at the moment, don't ignore the feelings of hurt and pain. Take some time to read through the psalm again, either quietly to yourself or aloud if you prefer. Focus particularly on verses 5,13 and 14. Ask God to make you strong enough to cope with the hassles in your life.

DAYZD 43 & 44

PSALM 126

THERE ARE CHRISTIANS WHO TRY TO KEEP ONE FOOT IN THE CHURCH AND THE OTHER IN THE WORLD. THERE ARE CHRISTIANS WHO HAVE GIVEN UP THEIR FAITH – FIGHTING THE GOD WHO CALLS THEM BACK, BUT UNHAPPY WITH THE WORLD'S BARGAINS. THERE ARE ALSO CHRISTIANS WHO HAVE LEFT GOD, ONLY TO RETURN RESTORED WITH REAL JOY AND HAPPINESS.

The joy of return is the theme of this psalm – the return of God's people to their own land. It is a testimony to the great work of God, making others stop and say 'Whoa!' (v 2). There's a spiritual principle at work here: God rewards us when we mean business. Sometimes there's no way round it – we have to sow in tears (vs 5a,6a). For 'sow' read 'repent, pray, obey ...' But the result will be a harvest causing joy (vs 5b,6b).

REAL JOY AND HAPPINESS.

We must not reject God in order to test him. But let's remember: coming back and making up can be great! He is someone who doesn't keep a record of what we have done against him. When we ask for forgiveness, he gives it completely.

ACTION

• LOOK AT VERSE 3. CAN YOU RELATE TO IT? HAVE YOU GOT VALUABLE MEMORIES OF 'GREAT THINGS' GOD HAS DONE FOR YOU?

PSALM 147

IF YOU LISTEN TO HEBREW MUSIC YOU'LL QUICKLY REALISE HOW MUCH THEY KNEW ABOUT PRAISE. THERE'S A REAL BEAT AND LIVELINESS HERE THAT COMES ACROSS EVEN THROUGH THE WRITTEN WORDS.

Psalm 147 is a lesson in a nation's praise. We are given two reasons to praise God – he deserves it, and it's fun (v 1)! The rest of the psalm outlines some reasons and events that show his worthiness. Try to spot which verses the following causes for praise are mentioned in:

He provides.
He protects.
He gets involved.
He's fair.
He's powerful.
He loves his people.
He guides.
He's in control.

Now work out your own list of reasons for praising God:

Remember, God is to be praised for who he is as well as what he has done!

• SING OR LISTEN TO YOUR FAVOURITE SONG OF PRAISE. THINK ABOUT THE REASONS WHY YOU LIKE IT SO MUCH? HOW DOES IT HELP YOU WORSHIP GOD BETTER?

PSALM 2 & HEBREWS 1:1-5

THE JEWS EXPECTED A MESSIAH, OR SAVIOUR. ALL THEIR HOPES WERE PINNED ON HIS COMING. IN A POLITICALLY THREATENED SITUATION THEY WANTED A KING TO FREE THEM FROM OPPRESSION; TO BEAT BACK THEIR ENEMIES (WHETHER BABYLONIAN, PERSIAN, ROMAN OR WHOEVER).

Psalm 2 describes an earthly king, but it also foretells a saviour sent by God. The writer of the letter to the Hebrews picks up verse 7 of the psalm and applies it to Jesus. He is the one who will lead the chosen people and rule the nations (Psalm 2:8 and 9; Hebrews 1:2).

No earthly king could reveal God so clearly as his Son. That's why Jesus said, 'He who has seen me has seen the Father'.

JESUS' KINGSHIP IS BASED ON LOVE, NOT FORCE.

When Jesus came to earth, how did he actually use his kingly power? Tick the right answer:
• He threw the Romans out of Israel.
• He took over all the governments of the world.
• He exterminated everyone who had sinned.
• He gave up his power to die for our sins.

Jesus' kingship is based on love, not force. What does this say to people in positions of power in the world? What does this say to us when we are in positions of power or influence.

ACTION

• SPEND SOME TIME PRAYING FOR CHRISTIANS IN POSITIONS OF POWER OR INFLUENCE, EG CHRISTIAN MPS, OR DIPLOMATS. PRAY THAT THEY WILL LOVINGLY BUT FIRMLY STAND UP FOR WHAT IS RIGHT.

PSALM 22:1-18 & MARK 15:34

JESUS CHRIST FULFILLED 330 PROPHECIES WRITTEN IN THE OLD TESTAMENT AT LEAST 400 YEARS BEFORE HIS BIRTH. THE ODDS AGAINST THAT ARE PHENOMENAL – EVEN LONGER THAN THE CHANCE OF WINNING THE NATIONAL LOTTERY ON THE FIRST ATTEMPT WITH JUST ONE TICKET! PSALM 22, IN THE LIGHT OF AFTER-EVENTS, SOUNDS TO US LIKE AN ECHO OF THE SUFFERINGS OF JESUS CHRIST AS RECORDED IN HE GOSPELS. JESUS HIMSELF QUOTED ITS FIRST VERSE IN MARK 15:34, JUST TO BRING THE PARALLEL HOME.

In exact ways God was warning his children what to expect – that the Son was sent to suffer. It wasn't a mistake; it was part of the total plan. Jesus the Son had to suffer to save mankind: to pay the penalty for our wrongdoing.

Find the prophecy and its fulfilment:
1. Verse 7 and 8 link with Mark 15:29-31.
2. Verse 18 links with Mark 15:24.
3. Verse 15 links with John 19:28.

Some people think that Jesus' death shows that he failed in his task. How do these Bible verses show they are wrong?

ACTION

• HEAR MORE ABOUT JESUS' PROPHECIES IN *READ THIS ... JOHN'S GOSPEL*, WELL OUTPOURED DESIGN, BY HODDER & STOUGHTON.

CHECK OUT

PSALM 40 & HEBREWS 10:17

HERE'S ANOTHER FULFILLED PROPHECY ABOUT JESUS. WE'VE SEEN HIM AS THE KING AND RULER (PSALM 2); WE'VE SEEN HIM AS THE ONE WHO SUFFERED FOR US (PSALM 22). NOW WE SEE HOW HE COMPLETES THE OLD TESTAMENT LAW.

THE ONE WHO SUFFERED FOR US.

The Law of God was revealed to Moses, and added to by years of Jewish religious practice. The Law is honoured in Psalm 40, and put in its place in Hebrews 10 – check both of these Bible readings out.

The psalmist has a difficult task. He recognises that the sacrifices and offerings set out in the Law cannot save us because sinful people are not capable of keeping all God's commandments.

It's easier for the writer of Hebrews. He has seen that Jesus completes the law by giving the ultimate sacrifice for sins – himself. The guilt sacrifice of the Old Testament, which the priests had to keep repeating, becomes the love sacrifice of the New Testament. Jesus, instead of sacrificing animals, sacrificed himself (Hebrews 10:9,10).

ACTION

• WHAT DOES IT MEAN TO YOU THAT JESUS HAS PAID THE PENALTY FOR YOUR SINS?

• READ PSALM 119.

DAYZD 49

PSALM 110 & HEBREWS 5:1-10

IMAGINE WHAT IT WOULD BE LIKE IF YOU COULD COLLECT ALL THE POWER, WEALTH, INFLUENCE AND IMPORTANCE OF ALL THE KINGS THERE HAD EVER BEEN, AND PILE IT ALL UP IN A HEAP. WELL, FAR ABOVE ALL THAT IS THE POWER, RICHES, IMPORTANCE AND INFLUENCE OF THE KING OF ALL KINGS, JESUS. THE ENEMIES OF JESUS ARE PUT UNDER HIS FEET, THE SIGN OF COMPLETE DEFEAT AND SUBMISSION.

He's also the last word in priests. To the Jews, Melchizedek stood for all the priests who offered sacrifices for sins on their behalf. But Jesus was both priest and sacrifice, the perfect, once-and-for-all offering for sins. Although he had the power to avoid it, he still chose to die and take the punishment for what we had done wrong. He's even greater than Melchizedek, the 'super-priest'! Jesus is King of Kings, Priest of Priests.

ACTION

• CHECK OUT HEBREWS 5:8. JESUS WAS AND IS THE ALL-POWERFUL SON OF GOD. YET ON THE CROSS HE ALLOWED HIMSELF TO BECOME COMPLETELY HELPLESS. SPEND A FEW MINUTES THINKING ABOUT THE WONDER OF THIS AND THANKING GOD FOR IT.

HEBREWS 1:1-14

IF YOU ASKED ONE HUNDRED CHRISTIANS IF THEY SOMETIMES FIND IT TOUGH TO FOLLOW JESUS, CHANCES ARE NINETY-FIVE WILL SAY 'YES, AND THE OTHER FIVE ARE TELLING A LIE!' WE ALL FIND IT DIFFICULT AT TIMES TO HANG IN THERE. HAVE YOU EVER FELT LIKE GIVING UP ALTOGETHER?

The readers of this letter were wavering in their faith, probably because of persecution. So the author (we don't know who for sure wrote Hebrews) focuses straight in on Jesus – who he is (vs 2,3) and his credentials (vs 5-14), setting the scene for the whole book. It's a lesson for us too – to look first at Jesus and remember that he gives the 'oomph' to our own tired resources.

Jesus' status is defined in terms of his relationship with the Father: God's Son and God's Word (the way God communicates with us (v 2); God's co-worker in creation (vs 2,10); God's revelation of himself, and the one at God's right hand (v 3); given authority by the Father (vs 4-8); chosen by God (v 9). And the incredible, mind-blowing reality is that this same Jesus, who is far superior than the most powerful angel, knows about, cares about and loves YOU! Knowing that helps give us strength not to give up.

ACTION

• IN WHAT WAYS ARE WE LIKE JESUS IN OUR RELATIONSHIP WITH GOD, AND DO WE HAVE SIMILAR PRIVILEGES?

• READ VERSE 3 AGAIN. USE EACH PHRASE AS A STARTING POINT FOR PRAISE. YOU MAY FIND IT HELPFUL TO USE KEVIN PROSCH'S WORSHIP SONG 'HE BROUGHT ME TO HIS BANQUETING TABLE (HIS BANNER OVER ME)' AS A PRAISE TRIGGER.

WE HAVE READ ABOUT HOW JESUS IS HIGHER THAN THE ANGELS AND ANYTHING ELSE. TODAY THE AUTHOR OF HEBREWS REMINDS HIS READERS THAT THIS SAME JESUS WAS MADE A LITTLE LOWER THAN THE ANGELS, AND WAS HUMILATED AND KILLED. CHECK OUT VERSE 9 WHICH IS ONE OF THE ALL TIME CLASSIC VERSES IN THE WHOLE BIBLE. EVEN THOUGH JESUS LITERALLY WENT THROUGH HELL, HE CAME BACK TO LIFE AND IS NOW CROWNED WITH GLORY AND HONOUR.

JESUS LITERALLY WENT THROUGH HELL.

It's good to know that, no matter what we go through in life, we can tell Jesus about our experiences and know for sure that he understands. He was once flesh and blood and knows what it is like to be tempted, feel pain, be rejected and suffer injustice.

Becoming a leader is usually considered to be 'going up in the world'! For Jesus it meant coming down into the world. Jesus started where we are and led the way through suffering and death, to put the lid on Satan once and for all, and to reign with God.

Following Jesus may mean saying some of the things listed below:

• 'I'm going to stand by you because I understand the problems you're facing.'
• 'With God's help I will come through this hell I'm experiencing.'
• 'Death is horrible and I'm right to be sad when I'm faced with it. But with Jesus I know it's not the end!'
• 'I see my whole life as an attack on Satan's strongholds, in the world and in my own life.'

Tick those you can already hear yourself saying with confidence. Pray about those you can't. Tell God – as long as it's true! – that you want to follow Jesus all the way.

ACTION

• LISTEN TO 'TRUST', BY SIXPENCE NON THE RICHER FROM THEIR ALBUM *THE FATHERLESS*, AS A TRIGGER FOR WORSHIP.

DAYZD 52

HEBREWS 4:14-5:10

HAVE YOU EVER FACED A DIFFICULT SITUATION AND FELT THERE WAS NO ONE YOU COULD CONFIDE IN WHO WOULD UNDERSTAND, SYMPATHISE AND NOT BETRAY YOUR SECRET TO OTHERS?

EVER FACED A DIFFICULT SITUATION?

Jesus understands everything about the rough end of life (5:2,7,8), and whatever you tell him, he understands and even better than sympathy – he empathises with you! Check out this word in a dictionary and you'll see that empathy is far better than sympathy. What's more, no matter what you tell Jesus he will carry on loving you.

That's why he is the ideal High Priest, the go-between in the man/God relationship. But he not only understands our problems, he has already paid for our mistakes (v 9).

ACTION

• IF YOU HAVE STARTED TO KEEP A JOURNAL, WRITE OUT 4:16. WHEN THINGS GET TOUGH, READ IT - IT TELLS YOU THE BEST PLACE TO START COPING AGAIN!

HEBREWS 7:26-8:6

DAY'Z'D
54
FIFTY
FOUR

WHEN YOU WERE LITTLE, MODELS WERE SOMETHING YOU PLAYED WITH ALL THE TIME - TRAINS, PLANES, DOLLS, CARS, FARM ANIMALS ... THEY WERE REAL ENOUGH TO YOU THEN, BUT WERE STILL MODELS. IT WAS ONLY WHEN YOU GREW-UP AND MET THE REAL THING THAT YOU REALISED THE MODEL'S RESTRICTIONS!

Similarly, the Jewish priesthood was only a copy, or model, of what Jesus would do and be, as the true High Priest for all time. One of the main high priestly functions was to offer animal sacrifices for sin (their own and the people's) in obedience to God's laws (Leviticus 9:7).

Find at least three ways in which Jesus is greater than the model.

1.

2.

3.

ACTION

JESUS, THEN, IS THE HIGH PRIEST THAT MEETS OUR NEEDS (7:26). DO YOU NEED JESUS TO DO ANY OF THE THREE THINGS YOU HAVE NOTED? TELL HIM NOW.

DAY'Z'D 54

HEBREWS 9:1-14

THE OLD WAY FOR SINFUL MAN TO APPROACH GOD WAS THROUGH THE SHEDDING OF THE BLOOD OF SACRIFICED ANIMALS. THE HIGH PRIEST ALONE WAS PERMITTED TO PERFORM THE CEREMONY, ANNUALLY, ON EVERYONE'S BEHALF. THE TABERNACLE'S DESIGN EMPHASISED THE SEPARATION OF MAN FROM GOD (VS 6-8).

The New Way into God's presence is through the shedding of Jesus' blood. As well as acting as High Priest, Jesus was also the perfect sacrifice. Unlike earlier High Priests, he had no personal sin to pay for. His offering was totally on our behalf, his life for ours. Now we can come into God's presence. This is what the tearing of the temple veil meant when Jesus died (Matthew 27:51).

It is rare to hear of someone giving up their own life to save someone else. When it does happen it is usually in a war situation and is rewarded by a posthumous medal like a Victoria Cross. Or sometimes we hear of someone who dives into water to save a drowning person and they end up as the one who drowns.

Spend some moments to thank Jesus for dying in your place. Then imagine what it is like to walk boldly into the place where God is. Picture it in your mind ...

'IN HIS LIFE CHRIST IS AN EXAMPLE, SHOWING US HOW TO LIVE; IN HIS DEATH HE IS A SACRIFICE, SATISFYING FOR OUR SINS; IN HIS RESURRECTION, A CONQUEROR; IN HIS ASCENSION, A KING; IN HIS INTERCESSION, A HIGH PRIEST.'
MARTIN LUTHER.

DAYZD 55

HEBREWS 10:19-39

WHAT A LIFE-STYLE CHECKLIST IN VERSES 19-25!

Circle a number to show how you rate yourself on a scale of 1 to 5 (5 means excellent).

Sincere heart	1	2	3	4	5
Sure faith	1	2	3	4	5
Free of guilty conscience	1	2	3	4	5
Facing the future with confidence because of the hope you have	1	2	3	4	5
Trusting God to keep his promises	1	2	3	4	5
Helping others to be loving/do good	1	2	3	4	5
Meeting with and encouraging other Christians	1	2	3	4	5

So where is action or prayer needed? At this point, you could be feeling terrible because you've got a whole string of 1's! Well, you don't need to feel bad if you are wanting to change with God's help. That's one big step in the right direction!

You probably have never had to cope with the same problems as the Christians this letter is addressed to (vs 32-34). But other things can stress you into letting your life-style slip. Remember – God has a great reward for those who are patient and faithful (vs 35,36). Christ won it for us (1 Peter 1:3-5). So hang in there and improve!

ACTION

USE THE WORDS OF THIS WORSHIP SONG WRITTEN BY BRIAN DOERKSEN AS A PRAYER:

DON'T LET MY LOVE GROW COLD
I'M CALLING OUT,
'LIGHT THE FIRE AGAIN'
DON'T LET MY VISION DIE
I'M CALLING OUT,
'LIGHT THE FIRE AGAIN'

YOU KNOW MY HEART MY DEEDS
I'M CALLING OUT,
'LIGHT THE FIRE AGAIN'
I NEED YOUR DISCIPLINE
I'M CALLING OUT,
'LIGHT THE FIRE AGAIN'

I AM HERE TO BUY GOLD
REFINED IN THE FIRE
NAKED AND POOR,
WRETCHED AND BLIND, I COME
CLOTHE ME IN WHITE,
SO I WON'T BE ASHAMED
'LORD, LIGHT THE FIRE AGAIN!'

DAYZD 56

HEBREWS 11:1-16

HAVE YOU EVER BEEN CHALLENGED TO 'PUT YOUR MONEY WHERE YOUR MOUTH IS'? THE BIBLE IS FULL OF STORIES OF PEOPLE DOING JUST THAT - ACTING ON WHAT THEY SAID THEY BELIEVE ABOUT GOD. CHECK OUT THE FOLLOWING VERSES TO DISCOVER THE CONSEQUENCES? (VS 4,6,7,16).

The root of faith is what we believe about God – his power, love, holiness, reliability, etc.

Faith blossoms as we take these God-qualities at their face value and experience God providing all we need and keeping his promises. Even when the fulfilment of God's promises seemed impossible, these men of faith hung on. As a friend of mine often says 'God says it. I believe it. That settles it!'

Is God challenging you to do something you're not sure of, but which would really please him? Give your faith a chance to blossom by saying 'Yes'.

'PUT YOUR MONEY WHERE YOUR MOUTH IS'.

ACTION

• FAITH IS LOOKING BEYOND THE UNCERTAINTIES OF THE 'HOW?' TO THE CERTAINTY OF THE 'WHO?' AND TRUE WORSHIP IS ACTING IT OUT.

HEBREWS 11:23-40

HEROES OR HEROINES.

IF YOU HAD TO IDENTIFY THREE WELL-KNOWN PEOPLE THAT YOU LOOK UP TO OR REGARD AS HEROES OR HEROINES, WHO WOULD THEY BE? A SUCCESSFUL BUSINESSMAN LIKE RICHARD BRANSON MAYBE, OR SOMEONE FAMOUS FOR STANDING UP FOR THE POOR LIKE MOTHER THERESA? OR MAYBE A FAMOUS SPORTS STAR ...

Why do you think we are given such a gallery of heroes in this part of the Bible?

Perhaps it makes you feel inadequate. Well, don't assume these were very special people. They were ordinary people who sometimes failed, but who learned to trust their very special God. They played important parts in God's plan for his people, though they weren't always aware of it at the time. Sometimes it was really tough (vs 35-38). Their obedience and trust was their worship. They thought God was *worth* following.

Write a verse about *yourself* that could go between verses 38 and 39. Begin: 'It was faith that made me ...'.

• WHY NOT FIND OUT MORE ABOUT SOME OF THESE CHARACTERS, USING A BIBLE DICTIONARY OR THE CROSS-REFERENCES IN YOUR BIBLE?

• WHAT WERE YOU SURE ABOUT THAT YOU COULDN'T SEE (V 1)?

ON YOUR MARKS (V 1). AN ATHLETE REMOVES HIS TRACK-SUIT TO RUN MORE FREELY. ARE THERE ANY HABITS/ACTIVITIES/ATTITUDES WHICH HINDER YOU WORSHIPPING GOD?

The race (v 1). Try to put into your own words what this race is.

The hurdles (vs 5-11). The Christian life is more like a steeplechase than a 100m sprint; but hurdles are meant for leaping, not avoiding. The key to endurance is faith – that our loving Father puts to good use every setback that comes our way (vs 10,11). What is your biggest hurdle now?

THE KEY TO ENDURANCE IS FAITH.

The goal. An athlete keeps the finish line constantly in mind to spur him on. Sometimes our 'hurdles' loom so large, we can forget why we are running. Keep your eyes on Jesus. You'll take the hurdles in your stride and be spurred on to finish the race.

ACTION

• TODAY WE HAVE JUST READ SOME OF THE MOST MEMORABLE VERSES IN THE NEW TESTAMENT. IF YOU HAVE TIME, RE-READ THESE ELEVEN VERSES ALOUD. STOP AFTER EACH VERSE AND LET THE WORDS SINK IN. THEN PRAY AND ASK GOD TO HELP YOU REMEMBER AND LIVE IN THE LIGHT OF THESE WORDS OF SCRIPTURE.

DAYZD 59

HEBREWS 12:12-29

EVER BEEN INTO THE MOUNTAINS AND EXPERIENCED THE CONTRAST BETWEEN A STORM AND RADIANT SUNSHINE? IF SO, YOU'LL GRASP THE CONTRAST BETWEEN SINAI AND ZION (VS 18-24). A MOUNTAIN STORM IS FRIGHTENING, AWE-INSPIRING; YOU FEEL VERY VULNERABLE. LIST ANY WORDS USED WHICH SHOW THE ISRAELITES FELT THIS WAY AT SINAI.

AWE-INSPIRING:

What word in verse 23 emphasises the contrast of Mount Zion?

Pie in the sky when you die? No! Zion isn't just a symbol of heaven, but also of our relationship with God now. We don't have to approach him in fear if we come via the cross. We are already part of the unshakeable, indestructible heavenly kingdom (vs 23,28). We stand on solid ground.

Pray that others will see the Lord in you as this security affects the way you live (v 14).

ACTION

• IT'S A TOUGH MESSAGE. BE ON THE SIDE OF THE GOD OF ZION, OR FACE THE TERRIFYING GOD OF SINAI.

DAYZD 60

1 CHRONICLES 28:1-21

'THIS JOB'S REALLY GETTING TO ME.'
'I'LL NEVER GET IT SORTED.'
'EVERY TIME I SIT DOWN TO DO IT, I GET UP FOR A CUP OF COFFEE.'

'THIS JOB'S REALLY GETTING TO ME.'

Is there a task facing you which makes you feel like this? Solomon must have felt a bit fearful when faced with the prospect of building the temple. It probably didn't help that his dad really wanted him to do well (vs 2,9-11) and we all know how that feels!

How to get unstuck:
• Speak to God about it (v 9).
• Remember your commitment to God and his commitment to you (v 9)!
• Be clear that this task – big or little – is God's work for you at the moment (v 10).
• Use whatever resources and advice other people can give (vs 11-19).
• Know that God is with you (v 20).
• Don't be afraid or worried (v 20).
• And just begin!

ACTION

• LEARN VERSE 9 OR VERSE 20, AND REPEAT IT WHENEVER YOU GET STUCK.

CHECK OUT

1 CHRONICLES 29:23-25

AND 1 KINGS 4:20-34.

WHAT DID SOLOMON NEED EACH DAY?

- 1 KINGS 4:22,23
- 1 KINGS 4:29
- 1 CHRONICLES 29:24,25

GOD MET EACH NEED. HE SAW TO IT THAT SOLOMON HAD ENOUGH FOOD, MONEY, FRIENDS AND WISDOM. WHAT ARE YOUR GREATEST NEEDS AT THE MOMENT? REMEMBER WHAT YOU NEED AND WHAT YOU WANT MAY BE TWO DIFFERENT THINGS.

God met Solomon's needs; he can deliver yours too!

Pray for people and countries with enormous needs. Ask God to show you what your part is in his plan to meet these needs.
• Read Matthew 6:29-33 to see what Jesus promises you.

• Pray for wisdom for the leaders of all Countries.

ACTION

• SPEND SOME TIME IN WORSHIP THANKING GOD FOR PROVIDING ALL YOUR NEEDS. READ THROUGH THESE LYRICS AND THEN SPEND SOME TIME MEDITATING AND WHAT THESE WORDS ARE SAYING TO YOU:

YOUR LOVE LOOKS AFTER ME IT NEVER FAILS
YOUR WORD TAKES CARE OF ME
AND KEEPS MY MIND ON YOU
YOU ARE MAJESTIC THROUGH ALL THE EARTH
I AM YOUR SERVANT FOR THE REST OF MY DAYS
YOU ARE MAGNIFICENT, THE GOD OF GLORY
I'M GOING TO WORSHIP YOU FOR THE REST
OF MY DAYS
FOR THE REST OF MY DAYS
FOR THE REST OF MY DAYS

© 1991 Chris Falson Music/Maranatha Music. Admin by Copycare, PO Box 77, Hailsham, BN27 3EF. Used by permission.

DAYZD 62

1 KINGS 7:51-8:13,22-30

IT'S ALL DONE AND DUSTED! THE TREMENDOUS TASK GIVEN TO SOLOMON IS FINISHED.

There was no mistaking God's presence in his temple (vs 10,11). Solomon was moved to praise by the sheer glory of God!

What did Solomon praise and thank God for?

Verse 24:

Verse 23:

Verse 27:

List any promises God has made to you that have already been fulfilled:

List any that you cannot yet see being kept:

Thank God for keeping his promises, and pray about promises he is yet to keep. (If you cannot think of promises that God has made you, ask him to show you why.)

DONE AND DUSTED!

ACTION

• WHAT MIGHT PREVENT US EXPERIENCING GOD'S LOVE (V 23)? THIS IS A THEME THAT RUNS THROUGH THE BIBLE. CHECK OUT WHAT JESUS SAID IN JOHN 14:21-24.

DAYZD 63

CHECK OUT

1 KINGS 9:1-9

GOD DEMANDS OUR OBEDIENCE AND PROMISES HIS PROTECTION. THIS DOES NOT CHANGE. IF WE CHOOSE TO JUMP OUT OF GOD'S HANDS WE SHOULDN'T BE SURPRISED IF WE GET HURT! REMEMBER IF WE HAVE CHOSEN TO WORSHIP GOD, OBEDIENCE IS A PRACTICAL SIGN OF WORSHIP.

OBEDIENCE.

God lists seven things that will happen to his people if they stop following him. See if you can spot them all.

1.

2.

3.

4.

5.

6.

7.

What do you think are the results of disobedience for Christians today?

Ask God to show you where you are disobedient and ask him to help you worship him by obeying.

ACTION

TUCKED DEEP INSIDE
LORD,
I REMEMBERED WHAT YOU SAID.
I TUCKED YOUR WORDS DEEP
INSIDE MY HEART.
AND JUST WHEN I NEEDED THEM,
THERE THEY WERE!
IT WAS WONDERFUL, LORD.
THANK YOU FOR
KEEPING YOUR WORDS IN ME
SO THAT THEY HELP ME
TO CHOOSE THE RIGHT THING.
LORD,
I WILL NOT FORGET YOUR WORDS.
                    HALCYON BACKHOUSE.

CHECK OUT

1 KINGS 11:1-13

SEX WAS SOLOMON'S DOWNFALL. HE WASN'T SATISFIED WITH ONE WOMEN, OR EVEN ONE HUNDRED! WHAT'S MORE HE MARRIED WOMEN WHO WORSHIPPED OTHER GODS - SOMETHING GOD SPECIFICALLY TOLD HIM NOT TO DO. FOR A KING RENOWNED FOR HIS WISDOM - WHEN IT CAME TO SEX - HE WAS A TOTAL IDIOT! GOD HAD WARNED WHAT WOULD HAPPEN (V 2) AND SURE ENOUGH IT DID (VS 3,4). IT WASN'T REALLY THE LOVE OF 1,000 WIVES THAT UPSET GOD SO MUCH AS THE WORSHIP OF THREE DISGUSTING FALSE GODS. FOR EXAMPLE, ONE OF THEM MOLECH, WAS A GOD WORSHIPPED BY THE AMMONITES AND INVOLVED THE RITUAL KILLING OF CHILDREN BY THROWING THEM INTO A FIRE! IT'S INCREDIBLE THAT A MAN WHO KNEW SUCH BLESSING FROM THE TRUE GOD SHOULD GET INVOLVED IN SUCH SICK STUFF.

Verses 9-11 are a very sad end to Solomon's story, but notice God's mercy still shining through (v 12).

God's warning (v 2) still stands. Christians who live to please God and non-Christians who don't, will have problems in a boy/girlfriend relationship, let alone as marriage partners (see 2 Corinthians 6:14). That is because their lifestyle and priorities will be different. Chances are that a non-Christian will have a different view point on sex and many other important issues. Relationships and marriage aren't easy at the best of times, so ignoring God's guidelines is asking for trouble. God's rules are there for our own benefit – it's not that he is a killjoy. Like Solomon, we ignore God's warning at our peril.

Pray that you'll have wisdom to look for another Christian as a partner.

ACTION

THE CRUCIBLE FOR SILVER AND THE FURNACE FOR GOLD,
BUT THE LORD TESTS THE HEART OF THIS CHILD.
STANDING IN ALL PURITY,
GOD, OUR PASSION IS FOR HOLINESS,
LEAD US TO THE SECRET PLACE OF PRAISE.

JESUS, HOLY ONE,
YOU ARE MY HEART'S DESIRE.
KING OF KINGS, MY EVERYTHING,
YOU'VE SET THIS HEART ON FIRE.

FATHER TAKE THIS OFFERING,
WITH OUR SONG WE HUMBLY PRAISE YOU.
YOU HAVE BROUGHT YOUR HOLY FIRE TO OUR LIPS.
STANDING IN YOUR BEAUTY, LORD,
YOUR GIFT TO US IS HOLINESS;
LEAD US TO THE PLACE WHERE WE CAN SING.

1 KINGS 11:41-12:20

DECISIONS! DECISIONS! WHO DO YOU TURN TO FOR ADVICE - AND WHY?

A nasty shock. When his father died, Rehoboam set off for Shechem to be crowned king by the northern tribes. But he was faced with an ultimatum (12:3).

Help! Who did he turn to for advice (12:6,8)? Pity that God wasn't invited to the consultations!

'We're not playing.' Rehoboam got it wrong. He asked for trouble – and he got it (v 16)! Rehoboam was left as king of Judah only. David and Solomon's great kingdom was divided.

DECISIONS! DECISIONS! WHO DO YOU TURN TO FOR ADVICE - AND WHY?

DECISIONS! DECISIONS! WHO DO YOU TURN TO FOR ADVICE - AND WHY?

Pray about:
• any decision you have to take.
• any advice you have to give.

ACTION

• LOOK BACK TO 1 KINGS 11:11 TO SEE THE PROPHECY WHICH CAME TRUE IN 12:20. GOD WAS STILL IN CONTROL.

1 KINGS 12:25-13:3

EXIT KING REHOBOAM. ENTER KING JEROBOAM.

• Jeroboam's problem
He didn't trust the people to worship God in Jerusalem – in the kingdom of Judah in the south – and still be loyal to him as king (vs 26,27).

• How he set about finding a solution
Verse 28: 'After thinking if over ...' What would David have done (see 2 Samuel 2:1)?

• Jeroboam's solution
He set up new places of worship, with a phoney priesthood. (Look forward to 1 Kings 13:33,34 to read of Jeroboam's 'reward' for this.) This led the way to the worship of false gods, and a downward spiral away from God by Israel.

FALSE WORSHIP.

ACTION

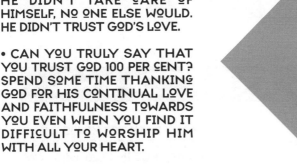

• 'LOOK AFTER NUMBER ONE.' JEROBOAM THOUGHT THAT IF HE DIDN'T TAKE CARE OF HIMSELF, NO ONE ELSE WOULD. HE DIDN'T TRUST GOD'S LOVE.

• CAN YOU TRULY SAY THAT YOU TRUST GOD 100 PER CENT? SPEND SOME TIME THANKING GOD FOR HIS CONTINUAL LOVE AND FAITHFULNESS TOWARDS YOU EVEN WHEN YOU FIND IT DIFFICULT TO WORSHIP HIM WITH ALL YOUR HEART.

1 KINGS 14:21-31

'COME ON, YOU GODS, COPY US. START HAVING SEX AND MAKE OUR LAND FERTILE!' THAT'S WHAT VERSE 24 MEANT!

WORSHIP GOD FOR THE REST OF YOUR DAYS.

To worship the God who created the universe wasn't powerful enough for the people of Judah! They borrowed a few religious customs from the local Canaanites – to help God along, so to speak.

How sick and sad it all was. A real insult to God.

Do we do the same sort of thing by mixing the advice of God with other 'gods'?

• 'Believe' in God and follow Mystic Meg?
• 'Trust' God to help us, but claim the credit for any success?
• 'Love' God but cling to our money instead of giving to those in need?
• Anything else?

If any of these are true for you, reflect on what you need to do to change and worship God alone.

ACTION

• TAKE SOME TIME OUT TO MEDITATE ON 'FOR THE REST OF MY DAYS', BY CHRIS FALSON. THINK ABOUT THE WORDS OF THE SONG. DO YOU BELIEVE IN WHAT THE WRITER OF THIS SONG HAS WROTE? ASK GOD TO HELP YOU TO 'WORSHIP GOD FOR THE REST OF YOUR DAYS'.

1 KINGS 16:29-17:6

DARK AND DANGEROUS DAYS

FIFTY YEARS ON AND FIVE EVIL KINGS LATER, WE MEET AHAB. NEVER BEFORE HAS THE COUNTRY SUNK TO SUCH DEPTHS (V 30). AHAB AND HIS FOREIGN WIFE JEZEBEL HAVE INTRODUCED A NEW RELIGION WHICH IS TOTALLY OPPOSED TO THE WORSHIP OF THE TRUE GOD. (BAAL IS THE PHOENICIAN GOD MELQART, THE GOD OF NATURE.) IT'S NO LONGER A CASE OF ADDING TO THE WORSHIP OF GOD, BUT OF DENYING IT COMPLETELY.

Desperate measures
Into this situation of great evil strides one of the greatest Old Testament prophets, Elijah. Unknown and unannounced he boldly states, 'No rain 'till I say so!' The people are about to learn which God really controls the forces of nature!

Meals on wings
The greatest miracle in the story of Elijah's provision is that those greedy black scavengers didn't gobble up their supplies (17:4-6).

Spend some time in prayer. Ask God to forgive the times you have taken worshipping him lightly. Think about how powerful the God who created and sustains the universe really is.

ACTION

• IF YOU HAVE BEEN KEEPING A JOURNAL, JOT DOWN SOMETHING WHICH REALLY SURPRISES YOU ABOUT GOD'S POWER FROM THIS PASSAGE.

• REMEMBER, NOTHING IS BEYOND GOD.

1 KINGS 18:1,2,17-41

'THE LORD IS GOD, THE LORD ALONE IS GOD!'

One man against 850 fanatical priests and priestesses, an angry king and an evil queen. This is perhaps one of the greatest and most dramatic confrontations of good and evil of all time. Stop and try to imagine the scene ... Elijah ought to have felt totally intimidated.

Re-read the passage – what impresses you most about Elijah?

☐ His patience. He stayed hidden for three years (v 1).
☐ His obedience to God (vs 1,2).
☐ His authority. It never occurred to Ahab to ignore Elijah.
☐ His humour (v 27).
☐ His confidence in God – even pouring water of the sacrifice.
☐ The simplicity of his prayer (vs 36,37).
☐ His ruthless destruction of evil (v 40). (Because of what this one man did, Baal worship never again became the official religion of the country.)
☐ Anything else?

Pray about what has most challenged you from this incident.

ACTION

• READ HABAKKUK 3:2 AND PRAY THIS PRAYER FOR YOUR VILLAGE/TOWN/CITY.

• USE A PRAISE TAPE TO LEAD INTO A SHORT TIME OF PRAISE AND WORSHIP – TRY LISTENING TO TRACKS LIKE; 'HE IS THE LORD AND HE REIGNS ON HIGH', (KEVIN PROSCH) OR 'OUR CONFIDENCE IS IN THE LORD', (NOEL RICHARDS).

DAYZD 70

2 CHRONICLES 31:20-3:23

INVASION!
MEANWHILE, BACK IN JERUSALEM AND SOME 250 YEARS ON FROM KING REHOBOAM, WE FIND THE PEOPLE BESIEGED, WITH DEFEAT A NEAR CERTAINTY.
BUT ALL IS NOT LOST! THEY HAVE A KING WHO TRUSTS GOD AND WHO FOLLOWS THE ADVICE OF AN OUTSTANDING PROPHET OF GOD (31:20, 32:20). NO ENEMY COULD WITHSTAND SUCH A COMBINATION.

DON'T PANIC !

DON'T PANIC !

In the face of doom and destruction, what does Hezekiah do?

1. ....(vs 3,4)
2. ....(v 5)
3. ....(v 6)
4. ....(v 6)
5. ....(v 7)

ACTION

• ARE YOU FEELING ATTACKED OR THREATENED OR STRESSED IN ANY WAY - BY FEARS, TROUBLES, DANGERS OR PROBLEMS? WRITE DOWN WHAT YOU CAN LEARN FROM HEZEKIAH.

2 KINGS 17:1-23

YESTERDAY, TRIUMPH; TODAY, TRAGEDY. WE'VE PUSHED THE 'FAST FORWARD' BUTTON PAST 170 YEARS AND ELEVEN WICKED KINGS OF ISRAEL. HOSHEA IS NOW KING. IT HAS TAKEN NINE YEARS BUT EVENTUALLY GOD'S PATIENCE WITH ISRAEL HAS RUN OUT AND THEY ARE OVERRUN BY SHALMANESER. ALL THE PEOPLE ARE TAKEN AS PRISONERS TO ASSYRIA.

Verses 7-19 give a catalogue of Israelite disobedience through the 240 years from Solomon to Hoshea. Out of the many reasons given here for God's anger, which do you think were the most serious wrongs?

Are there things in your life that are trying God's patience? Why not ask for his forgiveness now – and for his strength to put things right? Psalm 51 is a good psalm to read when you are sorry about something.

ACTION

• 'I KNOW PRACTICE MAKES PERFECT, LORD, SO I'LL BE CAREFUL WHAT I PRACTISE.'

• LISTEN TO 'CRUICIFIED' BY CHRISTAFARI FROM THE ALBUM *SOULFIRE*, AS A TRIGGER FOR PRAISE.

2 CHRONICLES 34:1-28

HILKIAH THE HERO! WE DON'T KNOW HOW OR EXACTLY WHERE BUT HILKIAH THE PRIEST MAKES THE AMAZING DISCOVERY OF GOD'S BOOK WHICH HAD DISAPPEARED YEARS EARLIER (VS 14,15). 'THE BOOK OF THE LAW' WAS THE FIRST FIVE BOOKS OF OUR BIBLE, GENESIS TO DEUTERONOMY.

People at that time had no written record of God's words or deeds. A dim memory was preserved by some of the prophets and priests (now largely ignored) and in the temple sacrifices (now usually neglected).

King Josiah's so excited that he stops everything to listen (v 18). But bad news (v 19)! All is not well. Why (v 21)?

Read 2 Timothy 3:15-17, and thank God that we can hear him speaking directly to us through the words of the Bible. Pray for:
• those banned from owning a Bible
• those with no translation in their language
• the work of the Bible Society and Wycliffe Bible Translators
• those who are not allowed to meet with other Christians to worship God.

ACTION

• FIND OUT IF YOUR CHURCH SUPPORTS ANY MISSIONARIES. MAKE TIME ON A REGULAR BASIS TO PRAY FOR THEIR NEEDS.

• PRAY WITH THANKS THAT WE LIVE IN A COUNTRY WHERE WE ARE FREE TO WORSHIP GOD, EG NO GOVERNMENTAL RESTRICTIONS. PRAY FOR FORGIVENESS THAT WE OFTEN DECLINE TO TAKE UP THIS OFFER.

JEREMIAH 1:1-3, 7:1-15

TRUE OR FALSE?
'GOD WILL SAVE ME AND ALL THE PEOPLE OF JERUSALEM BECAUSE WE WORSHIP IN HIS TEMPLE AND HE CANNOT POSSIBLY DESTROY IT.'

SAVE ME.

This is what everybody in Jerusalem said (7:4,10,11). False! Check out what Jeremiah said in verses 5-13.

True or false?
God will save me because:
• I have been baptised.
• I have been confirmed.
• I read my Bible and pray each day.
• I asked Jesus to be my Lord.

The first three are completely false, but this is what many people believe today. The last one is okay as far as it goes but what would Jesus reply?

(Check out Matthew 7:21 to find out.) Are you doing what Jesus would want you to do? Ask him to help you.

ACTION

• A HYPOCRITE: SOMEONE WHO PRETENDS TO BE WHAT HE/SHE ISN'T.

• ASK GOD TO POINT OUT ANY AREAS IN YOUR LIFE WHERE YOU PRETEND TO BE SOMETHING YOU KNOW YOU'RE NOT. ASK FOR HIS STRENGTH TO CHANGE.

• SPEND SOME TIME IN WORSHIP. TRY LISTENING TO 'COME INTO MY LIFE', CAPITAAN (FROM THE ALBUM, *DRIFTWOOD*, 1995, ICC).

2 CHRONICLES 36:1-12

DISASTER APPROACHES!

CHANCES ARE THAT YOUR FIRST REACTION TO THIS PASSAGE WAS ... 'BORING! JUST A SERIES OF NAMES AND FIGURES ... NOTHING WHICH RELATES TO ME TODAY.'

BORING !

Take a second look. These verses cover:
• A hectic twelve-year period.
• Five godless kings (an average reign of about two years per king!).
• Devastating raids by two great nations.
• A twelve-word summary of the entire book of Jeremiah (v 12).

Try re-reading these verses, imagining you lived in Jerusalem at the time. Think about what life would have been like for you. Take a few minutes to think about this – you might like to write some notes describing how you're feeling and what you believe God is saying through the events around you.

Write down some of the serious problems facing your country today.

Pray that your country's problems will make your nation and its leaders turn to God.

ACTION

• 'TODAY WE STILL LIVE IN A "GODLESS" SOCIETY'. IN WHAT WAYS DO YOU THINK THAT THIS QUOTE IS TRUE?

• ARE THERE ANY WAYS IN WHICH THE COUNTRY YOU LIVE IN IS ACTING AGAINST GOD'S WISHES? DO YOU THINK PEOPLE STILL PUT OTHER 'GODS' BEFORE THE WISHES OF GOD? WHAT DO YOU THINK CAN BE DONE ABOUT IT?

CHECK OUT
JEREMIAH 26:1-16

DISASTER COMES CLOSER.
AMONGST THE SHORTEST
BOOKS IN THE WORLD WOULD
BE 'HOW TO MAKE AND
MAINTAIN FRIENDSHIPS' BY
JEREMIAH THE PROPHET!

Think about the following questions:

- What did Jeremiah say in the temple courts?

- What did the leaders actually take in from what he said?

- What did they want to do?

- Why did they behave like this? Because they felt angry and threatened. They were quite happy. They did not want to be challenged, so they tried to destroy the challenger.

- What is your view of them? Wait! Before you're too hard on them, answer the following:

Question: Are there any sins which you commit over and over again?

Question: Do you know they are condemned by God?

DISASTER.

Question: Why do you continue to commit them? With God's strength, you could root them out if you really wanted to.

Answer:

• AM I COMFORTABLE WITH MY SINS, OR WILL I RESPOND TO GOD'S CHALLENGE (V 13)?

2 CHRONICLES 36:11-21

READING THIS PASSAGE IS LIKE LISTENING TO A TOLLING FUNERAL BELL, OR THE RATTLE OF MACHINE-GUN FIRE. THERE'S SOMETHING TERRIBLY FINAL ABOUT IT.

A TOLLING FUNERAL BELL.

What verse do you think sums up the passage most devastatingly? Re-write it in your own the words.

Five sins of Zedekiah and his leaders are listed. Jot them down here:
1.
2.
3.
4.
5.

So the line of kings, which had begun with such hope over 500 years earlier, comes to an end in terrible despair. It looks as though it's the end of Judah.

God used the Babylonians to punish his people (v 17). If you feel distant from God at the moment, ask him to show you the reason.

ACTION

• IF YOU HAVE TIME CHECK OUT PSALM 137. THIS WAS WRITTEN AFTER THE JEWS HAD BEEN CONQUERED AND THE PEOPLE EXILED TO BABYLON. IT REFLECTS THEIR FEELINGS OF BITTERNESS AND DESPAIR.

• QUOTE: 'BEFORE A MAN CAN MOVE THE WORLD HE MUST FIRST MOVE HIMSELF.' *SOCRATES*

JEREMIAH 29:1-14

HOPE IN THE DARK
THERE THEY ARE. JEWISH PRISONERS CAPTURED BY NEBUCHADNEZZAR IN ONE OF HIS EARLY RAIDS ON JUDAH. LIVING IN A FOREIGN COUNTRY AND LONGING TO GO HOME, THEY RECEIVE A LETTER FROM JEREMIAH. 'SETTLE DOWN AND PRAY FOR THOSE TOWNS WHERE YOU ARE CAPTIVES.' DEFINITELY NOT THE EXPECTED ADVICE! BUT THERE'S MORE. SOME OF THE LOVELIEST VERSES IN THE ENTIRE BIBLE! TALK ABOUT ENCOURAGEMENT; TALK ABOUT HOPE; TALK ABOUT VERSES 10-14!

TALK ABOUT ENCOURAGEMENT; TALK ABOUT HOPE.

Are you worried about the future? List the things that you are most concerned about:

Now meditate on and memorise verses 11,12 and 13. Pray, thanking God for his perfect plans for your future.

ACTION

• 'NO MATTER HOW BAD THINGS GET YOU HAVE TO GO ON LIVING EVEN IF IT KILLS YOU.' *SHOLEM ALEICHEM.*

• 'GOODNESS IS STRONGER THAN EVIL; LOVE IS STRONGER THAN HATE; LIGHT IS STRONGER THAN DARKNESS; AND LOVE IS STRONGER THROUGH DEATH; VICTORY IS OURS THROUGH HIM WHO LOVES US.' *DESMOND TUTU.*

DAYZD 78

EZRA 1

WATCH OUT! GOD AT WORK!

WORSHIP GOD.

GOD PREPARES HIS PEOPLE.
IN EXILE THE PEOPLE HAVE TURNED BACK TO WORSHIP GOD, MEETING IN SMALL GROUPS TO PRAY AND LEARN ABOUT HIM. (IT WAS DURING THIS TIME THAT 'SYNAGOGUES' - THE WORD MEANS 'GATHERING TOGETHER' - FIRST APPEARED.)

God prepares a ruler (v 1).
It may have been a seventy year wait but freedom comes, exactly as promised.

God calls out some of his people (v 5). The temple task force set off. Not everyone is willing, or able, to go but the Bible doesn't condemn those who stay behind.

God gives his people a task (vs 2,3). Top priority – rebuild the temple. First and foremost God has to be honoured.

God provides ample resources (vs 4-6). When God gives us a job, he gives us all we need to do it.

Are there areas in your life which you are waiting for God to bring answers to? Commit them to him now

ACTION

• GOD IS STILL AT WORK TODAY. WE CAN TRUST HIM TO WORK FOR US AND WITH US READ MATTHEW 6:33) AND SPEND SOME TIME IN PRAYER THANKING HIM.

EZRA 3

WHAT PRAISE! WHAT CELEBRATION! WHAT A DIN! AND JUST BECAUSE THE FOUNDATION STONE WAS LAID - PERHAPS IT'S JUST AS WELL THEY WEREN'T CELEBRATING THE COMPLETION OF THE TEMPLE! THEY PROBABLY SANG PSALM 136 (IN WHICH THE CHORUS IS REPEATED NO LESS THAN 26 TIMES!). TRUMPETS, CYMBALS AND EVERYONE SHOUTING AT THE TOPS OF THEIR VOICES. NOISY THEY MAY HAVE BEEN, BUT HALF-HEARTED THEY WERE NOT.

NOISY THEY MAY HAVE BEEN, BUT HALF-HEARTED THEY WERE NOT !

Think of some times when you have felt happy, eg when the football team you support scores a goal, at a concert with your favourite band, or when you have just received good exam results ... Chances are that you celebrated by shouting, cheering, jumping up and down, etc.

There are times when we celebrate what God has done for us when it is appropriate to be expressive in our reactions. If you were shouting or jumping up and down when you heard you had passed your exams – surely we should be shouting from the roof tops to celebrate the forgiveness from sins which Jesus has made possible!

Why not have a time of worship and praise now? Here are some suggestions to help you to get into some celebration praise:

ACTION

• MAKE A LIST OF YOUR TOP TEN REASONS TO PRAISE GOD.

• READ ALOUD A PSALM OF PRAISE FROM THE BIBLE - YOU COULD TRY 136, 145, 148 OR 150.

• LISTEN OR SING ALONG TO A PRAISE TAPE - THERE ARE SOME EXCELLENT ALBUMS AROUND INCLUDING SOME WHICH ARE IN HOUSE OR RAP STYLE.

• JESUS IS DESCRIBED AS THE FOUNDATION STONE, LAYING DOWN HIS LIFE FOR US (1 CORINTHIANS 3:11). SURELY THIS IS A REASON TO GIVE THANKS AND PRAISE!

EZRA 9:1-10:4

PRAYERFULLY AND COURAGEOUSLY THE TEMPLE WAS FINISHED. SEVERAL YEARS LATER, EZRA THE PRIEST WAS SENT TO SEE IF THE LAW OF GOD WAS STILL BEING OBSERVED. IT WASN'T.

Ezra discovered that the leaders and many of the people had married women who were not believing Jews (v 1). This was serious (look back to 1 Kings 11:1-3), and Ezra feared for the survival of Israel (v 14).

Ezra's reaction to the sinfulness of the people is surprising and interesting. Instead of getting angry with the people or telling God to punish the offenders, he repented as if he had committed the sin. Why do you think that he did that?

Ezra prays and weeps on behalf of the sinful people. What was the result (10:1-4)?

Think of a Christian group to which you belong. Are there problems there? If so, pray for forgiveness. Include:

• confession (vs 6,7,10,13)
• reasons why things have gone wrong (vs 10,12)
• thankfulness for God's goodness (vs 8,9).

ACTION

'GREAT SPIRIT, HELP ME NEVER TO JUDGE ANOTHER UNTIL I HAVE WALKED IN HIS MOCCASINS FOR TWO WEEKS.' *SIOUX INDIAN PRAYER.*

THINK ABOUT THIS QUOTE. WHOSE MOCCASINS DO YOU NEED TO WALK IN?

GOD SPEAKS TO US (8:1-3). IN A SPEECH TO THE HOUSE OF LORDS IN 1986, BARONESS TRUMPINGTON SPOKE ON 'EXPENSES PAID TO CHILD MINDERS'.

'There has been much confusion on this matter,' she said, noticing that several members of the Lords appeared to be frowning or surprised. She spoke for a further five minutes, warming to her theme until the expressions on the faces of the men and women around her triggered an embarrassing thought. She suddenly stopped. 'My Lords,' she said, 'I have been speaking on the wrong subject!'

The debate was supposed to be about an amendment to the Social Security Bill. She later admitted that she had brought along the wrong notes – hence the inappropriate speech.

Why do you think the people asked for the book of the Law of Moses (the Pentateuch, the first five books of the Old Testament) to be read out from start to finish without interruption? (This would have taken around six hours!)

Why were the laws God gave to Moses an appropriate speech to listen to?

We speak to God (9:6-33).
Ezra teaches and the people immediately respond in a prayer. How would you summarise it?

Which verse is the best description of your own feelings about God at the moment?

ACTION

• THINK FOR A FEW MINUTES ABOUT ALL GOD HAS DONE FOR YOU. DESPITE ALL THE TIMES YOU'VE LET HIM DOWN, HE'S GONE ON HELPING YOU AND PROTECTING YOU. HE'S INCREDIBLE!

• THANK AND PRAISE HIM AND CONFESS ANYTHING YOU NEED TO PUT RIGHT.

• WHY DON'T YOU READ THROUGH THROUGH A WHOLE BOOK OF THE BIBLE OVER THE NEXT COUPLE OF MONTHS, EG JOHN'S GOSPEL TO SHOW HOW SERIOUS YOU ARE TO SPEND TIME WITH GOD.

CHECK OUT

1 THESSALONIANS 4:13-5:2

PAUL HAD LEFT THE NEW GROUP OF BELIEVERS IN THESSALONICA AFTER ONLY A FEW WEEKS WITH THEM. THEY WERE GROWING IN THEIR NEW FAITH BUT SOME THINGS STILL PUZZLED THEM. SO THEY HAD ASKED HIM FOR FURTHER TEACHING. IN PARTICULAR, THEY WANTED TO KNOW MORE ABOUT CHRIST'S RETURN. WHEN WOULD IT HAPPEN? WHAT WOULD HAPPEN TO CHRISTIANS WHO HAD DIED BEFORE JESUS CAME BACK?

But Paul refuses to go into any details of time or place. He will tell them only what Jesus has taught him (v 15a). Verse 13 shows us the purpose of Paul's teaching. He is not aiming to satisfy people's curiosity, but to strengthen the church. So he stresses the most important points:

• Our future is to be with the Lord (v 17).
• Jesus will return suddenly, so we should always be prepared for him (5:2).

The Bible will not give us an answer to every question we have. What it will give us is a 'God's eye view' on the most important things in life. Studying the Bible teaches us general principles and guidelines to follow. With the help of the Holy Spirit and other Christians, we can work out the details for ourselves.

ACTION

• ABOUT WHICH SUBJECTS DO YOU FEEL YOU NEED MORE TEACHING?

• HERE ARE A NUMBER OF WAYS IN WHICH YOU CAN GET HELP WITH YOUR SPIRITUAL QUESTIONS:

• READ/LISTEN TO BIBLE STUDY BOOKS/CASSETTES, SUCH AS THE DAYZD SERIES.
• JOIN A BIBLE STUDY GROUP.
• ASK A CHRISTIAN FRIEND.
• ASK OUR MINISTER.
• READ A CHRISTIAN BOOK.
• GO TO A YOUTH CAMP, CONFERENCE OR SPECIAL EVENT.

• WHY NOT CONTACT SCRIPTURE UNION'S MARKETING DEPARTMENT AND ASK TO BE SENT A CATALOGUE OF THEIR NUMEROUS RESOURCES. DID YOU KNOW THAT SCRIPTURE UNION PUBLISHES BOOKS, MAGAZINES, BIBLE READING GUIDES, AUDIO CASSETTES AND VIDEO'S - AS WELL AS ORGANISING EXCELLENT HOLIDAYS FOR YOUNG PEOPLE ?

MATTHEW 25:31-46

THIS PARABLE CAN BE DESCRIBED AS ONE OF THE MOST UNNERVING PASSAGES IN THE NEW TESTAMENT! WHICH OF US DARES TO COUNT OURSELVES AMONG THE 'SHEEP' WHO WILL BE CALLED TO CHRIST'S 'RIGHT SIDE' WHEN HE RETURNS TO JUDGE US? WE SEE SO MANY HUMAN NEEDS ALL AROUND US; SURELY WE AREN'T EXPECTED TO MEET THEM ALL?

Two things to remember:

1. The 'righteous' were not aware that in serving other people they had been serving Christ himself. It just 'came naturally' because they had the life of Christ in them. Matthew 12:33-35 makes this clearer: the way we live is the fruit of what's in our hearts. A good heart produces acts of love, and a bad heart produces evil acts. But Christ can make our bad hearts into good ones!

2. If you're overwhelmed by all the need in the world, remember there were many needy people in Jesus' day too – just think of all the socially disadvantaged people who are mentioned in the gospels! Jesus doesn't say that each of us should try to meet every need all on our own. We are to start where we are, and help those we can help. And as the 'body of Christ', we're supposed to work together!

If you have been keeping a journal, jot down the passage of the Bible which you find most challenging and then write what your response to this should be.

ACTION

• 'OUR ATTITUDE TO OTHERS IS OUR ATTITUDE TO CHRIST'. WHAT NEEDS CHANGING IN YOUR ATTITUDE TO OTHERS?

DAYZD 84

'GOD WILL NEVER ACCEPT ME UNLESS I LIVE A PERFECT LIFE.' DOES PART OF YOU SECRETLY AGREE WITH THAT? IT'S PROBABLY THE MOST COMMON MISTAKE AMONGST CHRISTIANS.

The believers in Galatia had been taught that only by obeying the very demanding Jewish laws could they be okay in God's sight. Then they heard the Good News that Jesus had died to pay the penalty for their sins. Now they no longer had to live by a set of rules; God's Spirit would live in them and change them. They were free!

But they soon forgot this truth and began to try earning their way into heaven again (v 3). So here Paul uses the Old Testament scriptures to put them right. Even Abraham, the father of the Jewish nation, was accepted by God not because he kept God's laws, but because he had faith in God (vs 6-9). The Good News is that it's because God accepts us through Christ that we can live a new life – not the other way around!

Check out Paul's motive for correcting the Galatians – he's not trying to prove them wrong and himself right, but to lead them back to God's truth (see 1:11,12). And his method is to remind them of what it was that first brought them to Jesus (3:2).

• ARE YOU GUILTY OF PRESENTING CHRISTIANITY AS THOUGH IT WERE BAD NEWS INSTEAD OF GOOD NEWS?

• LISTEN TO 'TOUCH MY LIFE', FROM THE ALBUM *IT'S A SMALL WORLD*, SPRING *HARVEST PRAISE MIX 1995*, AS A TRIGGER FOR PRAISE.

DAYZD 85

PSALM 23

BIBLICAL MEDITATION IS NOT GOING INTO A TRANCE! IT'S A WAY OF LINKING BIBLE STUDY AND PRAYER - LETTING THE WORD OF GOD SINK INTO YOUR MIND AND HEART SO THAT IT CAN AFFECT YOU MORE DEEPLY. HERE IS AN EXAMPLE OF HOW YOU CAN MEDIATE ON A BIBLE PASSAGE.

Start by sitting or kneeling comfortably. Close your eyes and breathe deeply until you feel relaxed. Open your eyes and read through Psalm 23 two or three times until it starts to become familiar (you may already know this one pretty well!). Then choose one of the three methods below:

1. Pick a verse that stands out for you and let your thoughts roam around its meaning (a Scots preacher used to say, 'Put that on your tongue and suck it like a sweetie'!) After a few minutes write down your thoughts. Use these thoughts in your prayers.

2. The central message of the psalm is that God cares for us. Think back to times in your life when God's love has been very clear to you. Let your memories lead you into thanking him.

3. Choose one of the scenes mentioned in the psalm: the green fields and quiet waters, or the deep darkness of verse 4, or God's 'house'. Form a picture of the scene in your imagination, and place yourself in it. Concentrate on how you feel in that setting. Try to discover if God is saying anything to you through it. Then move into prayer.

ACTION

HERE ARE SOME OTHER PASSAGES YOU COULD USE FOR MEDITATION:
• MOST PSALMS, ESPECIALLY SHORT ONES SUCH AS 131, 133, 150.
• MATTHEW 6:9-13 (THE LORD'S PRAYER).
• ROMANS 8:31-39 (A GREAT STATEMENT OF GOD'S LOVE).
• REVELATION 21:1-7 (THE PROMISE OF A NEW WORLD).
• JOHN 1:1-14 (JESUS THE ETERNAL WORD OF GOD).
• EPHESIANS 1:3-10 (GOD'S PLAN FOR US).

EXPERIMENT WITH YOUR OWN WAYS OF MEDITATING ON THEM!

• IF YOU FIND IT HELPFUL PLAY SOME WORSHIP MUSIC IN THE BACKGROUND AS YOU FOCUS ON THE VERSES YOU HAVE READ.

2 CORINTHIANS 3:1-18

WORD STUDY ALLOWS US TO TRACE KEY WORDS AROUND THE BIBLE AND BUILD UP A FULLER PICTURE OF THEIR MEANING BY SEEING THEM USED IN DIFFERENT WAYS. THIS IS WHAT YOU HAVE BEEN DOING WITH THE WORD 'WORSHIP' IN *DAYZD*.

Today's reading (2 Corinthians 3:1-18) gives us a chance to study the word 'glory' (or 'splendour' in some translations) from just one passage. Paul is contrasting the old covenant (God's agreement with the Jews) with the new covenant (our relationship with Christ).

What does the word 'glory' mean to you? Spend a couple of minutes writing down your ideas on it.

• The old way brought death, because it condemned everyone who couldn't keep God's Law – and no one could (v 5b)!
• The new way brings life, because through Jesus we can be forgiven, and his Spirit lives in us to make us holy (v 6).

The old way had a physical glory (v 7):
• When Moses was given the Law his face literally shone so brightly that he had to cover it (Exodus 34:29-35).
• Ezekiel saw a vision of God as a man-shaped figure in an unbearably bright light, described in one translation as 'the likeness of the glory of the Lord' (Ezekiel 1:26-28).
• Daniel saw a similar vision to that of Ezekiel, in which a figure in brilliant light represented the presence of God (Daniel 10:4-8).

But the new covenant takes away the barrier between us and God (2 Corinthians 3:13,14). We can, as it were, take off our mask and begin to 'look God in the face'. So we acquire a spiritual glory. The light of God shows, not on our faces, but in our hearts and lives.

ACTION

• OTHER BIBLE WORDS YOU COULD STUDY:
'HOLINESS', 'LOVE', 'JUSTICE', 'SALVATION'. USE A CONCORDANCE - A DICTIONARY OF BIBLE REFERENCES - TO FIND THEM. *CRUDEN'S POCKET CONCORDANCE* IS A GOOD ONE TO START WITH. ALTERNATIVELY THERE ARE SEVERAL DIFFERENT 'STUDY BIBLES' AVAILABLE WHICH EXPLORE THE MEANING OF THE TEXT. VISIT A LOCAL CHRISTIAN BOOKSHOP AND HAVE A BROWSE THROUGH WHAT'S AVAILABLE. IF YOU CAN'T AFFORD A STUDY BIBLE, WHY NOT TAKE DOWN THE DETAILS OF THE ONE YOU LIKE BEST AND ASK FOR IT AS A BIRTHDAY OR CHRISTMAS PRESENT.

LUKE 10:38-42 & JOHN 11:1-44, 12:1-8

YES, TODAY'S READINGS ARE QUITE LONG, BUT THEN YOU NEED TO SPEND TIME WITH PEOPLE TO GET TO KNOW THEM! THE WHOLE OF THE BIBLE IS ABOUT GOD'S DEALINGS WITH PEOPLE, SO LOOKING AT PARTICULAR PEOPLE IS A GOOD WAY TO LEARN.

To lighten the load a bit, we've spread this study of Mary and Martha over two days. For today, just write down your impressions of the two women from the passages you've read. Jot down chapter and verse references to help you find your way back to the bits that struck you particularly.

WORDSWITHOUTSPACEMAKESNOSENSE
WORDSWITHOUT SPACE MAKENOSENSE
WORDS WITHOUT SPACE MAKE NO SENSE

LIFEWITHOUTSPACEMAKESNOSENSE
LIFEWITHOUT SPACE MAKESNOSENSE
LIFE WITHOUT SPACE MAKES NO SENSE

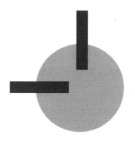

MAKE SPACE FOR GOD
EVEN IN THE FAST LANE.
GEORGE WHITE

LUKE 10:38-42 & JOHN 11:1-44,12:1-8

FIRST, LOOK BACK AT YOUR NOTES ON THE PASSAGES YOU READ YESTERDAY TO REFRESH YOUR MEMORY. AS YOU MAY HAVE GATHERED BY NOW, MARY, MARTHA AND THEIR BROTHER LAZARUS WERE AMONG JESUS' BEST FRIENDS. HE OFTEN WENT TO THEIR HOME AT BETHANY, JUST OUTSIDE JERUSALEM, WHEN HE NEEDED TO GET AWAY FROM THE CROWDS.

• Martha was the 'practical' sister, always coming out with the plain facts (see John 11:39) and taking on the everyday tasks (John 12:2). She got on with the work any ordinary woman would be expected to do in those days. We can see that the family weren't rich, or they would have had servants to do the work.

• Mary on the other hand took an unusual role for a woman – sitting at the feet of a 'rabbi' or religious teacher (Luke 10:39). Only men were supposed to do that! Indeed the rules about men and women mixing were so strict that a man wasn't supposed to greet his own wife in the street!

• Mary was dreamy (so sunk in grief for Lazarus that she didn't hear Jesus arrive), emotional and impulsive. She 'wasted' a whole jar of expensive perfume – I wonder what Martha the good housewife thought of that!

But Jesus defended Mary against those who grumbled about her (Luke 10:42, John 12:7). Love for him was the centre of her life and, compared to that, nothing else mattered.

ACTION

• THINK ABOUT WHETHER YOU ARE MORE LIKE MARY OR MARTHA? WHAT CAN YOU LEARN FROM EACH OF THEM?

• OTHER CHARACTERS TO STUDY: THE DISCIPLES PETER, JAMES AND JOHN; PAUL'S CO-WORKER BARNABAS; KING SAUL (A LOT TO READ HERE!); JACOB AND ESAU, AND MANY OTHERS. USE THE 'PEOPLE AND PLACES' SECTION OF A CONCORDANCE TO FIND THEM.

ROMANS 12:1,2

WORSHIP IS A HUGE SUBJECT TO LOOK AT - IT COVERS SO MANY DIFFERENT THINGS. TAKE SOME TIME NOW TO THINK ABOUT THE DIFFERENT ASPECTS OF WORSHIP YOU HAVE READ ABOUT IN *DAYZD*.

WORSHIP IS A HUGE SUBJECT.

If you have been keeping a journal, look back over your notes and then look at these questions. If you haven't been keeping a journal look at the questions anyway:

• What different ways of 'worship' have you learnt about through using *DAYZD*?

• What are the most exciting Bible verses you have read? Why?

• What are the most challenging Bible verses you have read? Why?

• How do you think you can start to worship God better?

• What do you still find difficult about worshipping God? Spend some time in prayer asking God to help you with these areas in your life.

ACTION

• CHECK OUT ROMANS 12:1,2. THIS VERSE REALLY SUMS UP WHAT *TRUE* WORSHIP IS ABOUT. SPEND SOME TIME MEDITATING ON THESE VERSES. PRAY THAT GOD WILL HELP YOU TO BE DEDICATED TO HIS SERVICE AND THAT YOU WILL LIVE YOUR LIFE IN A WAY THAT IS PLEASING TO HIM.

TO FIND OUT MORE ABOUT DECISION-MAKING AND KNOWING GOD'S WILL, WHY NOT READ *DAYZD: GUIDANCE?*

• WRITE INTO SCRIPTURE UNION AND TELL US WHAT YOU LIKED AND DISLIKED ABOUT *DAYZD*.

GET

DAY'ZD

AND YOU WON'T BE CONFUSED

- DOES GOD TALK TO NORMAL PEOPLE?
- ARE YOU A CHRISTIAN? GET A LIFE!
- I BELIEVE! WHERE TO NOW?
- SO WHAT'S RIGHT WITH SEX?

DAYZD GIVES IT TO YOU STRAIGHT FROM THE BIBLE.

90 DAYS FOR 90'S LIFE